The Elite ENTREPRENEUR

BESTSELLING BOOKS BY EPHREN TAYLOR

■

Creating Success from the Inside Out

Develop the Focus and Strategy to Uncover the Life You Want

The *Elite* ENTREPRENEUR

HOW TO MASTER THE 7 PHASES OF BUSINESS & TAKE
YOUR COMPANY FROM PENNIES TO BILLIONS

EPHREN W. TAYLOR

with Rusty Fischer

BENBELLA BOOKS, INC
DALLAS, TEXAS

BenBella

BenBella Books, Inc.
10300 N. Central Expy., Suite 400
Dallas, TX 75231
www.benbellabooks.com
Send feedback to feedback@benbellabooks.com

Printed in the United States of America
10 9 8 7 6 5 4 3 2 1

ISBN 978-1-935618-05-8

Editing by Brian Nicol
Copyediting by Lisa Miller
Proofreading by Erica Lovett
Cover design by theBookDesigners
Text design and composition by Neuwirth & Associates, Inc.
Printed by Bang Printing

Distributed by Perseus Distribution
perseusdistribution.com

To place orders through Perseus Distribution:
Tel: 800-343-4499
Fax: 800-351-5073

E-mail: orderentry@perseusbooks.com

Significant discounts for bulk sales are available. Please contact Glenn Yeffeth at glenn@benbellabooks.com or (214) 750-3628.

CONTENTS

The Elite ENTREPRENEUR

INTRODUCTION

How old are you right now? Thirty? Forty? Sixty? Twelve? Lots of people find it shocking the first time they hear my story and learn that I began focusing on business at the tender age of twelve. That's right—twelve—when most kids are riding bicycles, playing video games, and basically goofing around. Nobody's serious at age twelve, right? Maybe everyone else thought that way, but not me.

Why business? I figured out pretty early that I couldn't dance well, I couldn't sing a note, and I wasn't very good at sports, even though I did play high school football. Besides, a diagnosis of scoliosis ended my not-so-realistic chances of becoming an NFL pro.

I didn't want to go to work for someone else, and I wasn't raised to think the government owed me or my family anything. Because of my incredible parents, I knew I could achieve whatever I set my sights on, so I didn't listen to the clowns, the politicians, and the media personalities who tried to tell me anything different.

Like most kids my age, I loved video games. I loved

them so much I could pretty much master any game I got my hands on. Still can! By the time I was twelve, my parents were fed up with shelling out money for new games and stopped buying them.

I'll never forget the day my mother said, "Hey, Ephren, why don't you make your own video game?" At the time I thought it was a cruel joke, but I thought about it and said to myself, "Wow, that would be sort of cool. Instead of Super Mario, it could be Super Ephren!" So I took my mom up on the challenge. (In a way, I guess you could say I owe it all to Mom.)

I didn't have any experience programming video games—I was just twelve, after all! I didn't know anything about it; I just knew how to play the ones I had. So I went to the best sources of information I could find (and that I could afford, like the library), but to my surprise I *still* couldn't find any information on it. Then one day I was in a bookstore and a prophetic moment came to pass. I felt like a light was shining from the clouds when I came upon it: *How to Make a Video Game in 21 Days*. The book cost $50. While my parents didn't want to buy video games, they did always promote education and us pursuing our dreams. So, they bought the book for me, and I taught myself how to create a video game. I didn't even have a computer at the time—I had to use the ones at school.

I studied hard, worked on the school computers, found mentors to guide me, and eventually, I created my own game! No, I didn't have a college degree or even a high school diploma. I just did it. Then other kids wanted a copy of my game, and I realized I could make $10 apiece by burning copies. So I began selling my game, plus new ones I designed. I was in a very profitable business almost before I knew it. Was I too young to do that? Of course not! I simply did it!

I kept going. By age sixteen, I had won Microsoft's Teen TechFest Challenge and had started a job search engine for teens. I was building a business, raising money, putting together agreements with Walmart, Citigroup, Sprint, Target, the Air National Guard, and others. I got them to list their jobs on my search engine. And somehow I managed to keep up with my math, science, and English homework. I was a good student, *and* I was becoming hooked on business.

The Kauffman Center for Entrepreneurial Leadership in my hometown, Kansas City, offers an EntrePrep scholarship. I applied—and won. I was able to attend Kauffman, and the things I learned there took me to a whole new level and helped me build my business skills even more.

I picked up more mentors along the way. They taught me about growing a business, hiring and managing talent, preparing for and making presentations to investors, and a whole lot more. I personally raised more than $250,000 to grow my company.

And man, did we grow it!

An online job search engine, My First Dot Com Company, grew into an enterprise worth millions by the time I was seventeen. By nineteen, I retired and began helping my dad in a church he'd established. I took the donation and endowment monies and started managing them, investing them in homes for families within our own community. I used all the things I had learned to develop successful investment strategies—so successful I was named the Kansas Young Entrepreneur of the Year in 2002. I've continued to refine those strategies, and we still use them in our companies today, plus a few more I've picked up along the way. Those strategies helped me take a company public at age twenty-three (in fact, I've now taken three companies public, and I'm just twenty-eight).

Taking a company public the first time was a phenomenal feat, but nobody knew about it.

That all changed in 2007 when I published my first book, *Creating Success from the Inside Out,* which hit the *Wall Street Journal*'s bestseller list *twice*. It was also in the top five in a number of categories on Amazon.com and claimed the number nine spot on CEORead.com's top business books of 2008. Needless to say, my life has changed drastically since I wrote my last book. I've been on the *Today* show, the front page of CNN.com, ABC's *20/20*, and served as a regular correspondent on the Fox

Business Channel. Even more satisfying, I've received hundreds of letters from parents, students, and individuals who have been touched by the book. A gentleman from Norway emailed to thank me because he had read it and seen coverage on YouTube and decided to quit his job and start his own cooking line. He was successful—his cooking line was picked up by a store. The ability to influence people like that man and so many others was the reason we put the book out in the first place. And it's the reason why my team and I decided it was time for round two—another book!

You might be saying to yourself, so why a second book, Ephren? As I listened to people as I toured the country, I realized that my first book was very successful because it was a great inspirational story. Yet as great as that story was, I realized that what people really needed was training and more practical tips about exactly what it takes to become an entrepreneur. And that's why I've written *The Elite Entrepreneur*.

Everybody wants to be an entrepreneur. But do they really realize what it takes to be become one? Do they realize the sacrifices they've got to make and the energy they've got to put into it? There are so many misconceptions out there about what it takes. And most of what we need to know is not taught in the traditional classroom. We often have misconceptions about how it's going to be when we step into the entrepreneurial role, but I wanted to put something out there that really broke down the process step-by-step. I also want to share some of my life experiences, battles, and successes, as well as the obstacles my team and I have had to overcome. I feel information like this is needed now more than ever as America is coming out of the recession of 2008–2010, an economic slump that has touched and affected so many lives. For many people, the recession meant their Plan A just went out the door. Now it's time for Plan B—owning a business. People were laid off in unprecedented numbers, no matter where they were in their careers. Many people had to create those side jobs just to make ends meet. But how do you take that side job or that hobby or that additional income stream and turn it into a true business? That's what we're going to teach you to do in this book.

TRADITIONAL ENTREPRENEURS ARE FAILING! WE NEED ELITE ENTREPRENEURS!

The traditional entrepreneur is someone who had a dream and decided to jump in head first and go for it without a good understanding of the skills, resources, and strategies to make it happen. These entrepreneurs are failing because there is so much more competition via the Internet, a lack of bank lending, and fewer opportunities in general. When you read stories about the high rate of business failures, maybe 95 percent of the people you're reading about are these traditional entrepreneurs.

Then there is that rare breed—the Elite Entrepreneur. The guy or gal who can jump into nearly any type of industry, any type of product, and make something happen every single time. As you'll see, every failing entrepreneur has a different story and different reasons, while Elite Entrepreneurs share a certain formula and skill set that make it possible for them to adapt anywhere. People ask me all the time, "How did you transition from video games to consulting, and then to biofuels, real estate, publishing, and now, creating iPhone applications . . . and dominate whenever you come out?" Quite simply, because I've applied the same principles each time: being persistent and resourceful; connecting the dots and developing a vision for success.

I may be the general and the guy with the plan, but I also know the importance of always bringing in the right soldiers every time to make sure that mission is executed flawlessly. And Elite Entrepreneurs realize what their strengths are. They know what they know; but more important, they know what they don't know. They always surround themselves with people who can make things happen. Elite Entrepreneurs also have a mental state unparalleled and unlike any other. Other strengths include their ability to deal with challenges and see them as opportunities, their ability to tap dance when needed, and the ability to give the right perception and turn it into absolute reality. They're able to create a movement that motivates people and brings everything together in a winning formula.

In my experience, I've seen two major obstacles prevent most people from graduating to that next level of entrepreneurship and becoming Elite Entrepreneurs. The first is fear. In *Creating Success from the Inside Out,* we talked about "The Dark Hall of Fear" and how we can't eliminate fear but we CAN choose to control it and not live our lives bound by it. We can learn to recognize it, call it what it is, and deal with it. That is our choice. As with any emotional issue, the first step is to recognize how fear works in our lives and understand the ways it controls us. Fortunately, there are forces that are stronger, more powerful, and more positive than fear. One of these is faith. I am here to tell you that faith will overcome fear like light overcomes darkness.

Another obstacle that stops people from being Elite Entrepreneurs is the tendency to operate in their "comfort zone," to only seek opportunities that are familiar and local, right in their own backyard. I can't tell you how many times I've sat down to talk with entrepreneurs who say, "Ephren, I'm making a hundred thousand a year, but how do I make a million a year?" Truth be told, it takes the same amount of effort, time, and energy to make the million a year as it does to make the hundred thousand. The challenge is getting those entrepreneurs to break out of their comfort zone and break their addiction to working. They need to realize that, with that mentality, they aren't entrepreneurs, but just self-employed workers. They are simply employees of their own company and do not possess a true own-ership/elite entrepreneurial mindset. They're holding their own company back by managing with a control mentality. All of us have been there. What I realized in my own companies and in my own ventures is that I had to step back, to take a backseat sometimes and allow the person who can execute better step in. Tra-ditional entrepreneurs see their companies as their vision and their baby. They'll take it as far as they pos-sibly can, but in the end it will be stifled. On the other hand, Elite Entrepreneurs will bring in the right people and the right resources to accomplish the mission and grow their businesses to the best of their ability, even if it means they have to step aside and let it go.

employees of own company

THE 7 PHASES OF BUSINESS

Every business has a life cycle, but it's not as simple as "beginning, middle, and end." For one thing, successful business owners never want to think it might end, and who's to say when it all began?

Did Starbucks start the day the first coffee shop opened its doors in Seattle, or the first time founder and CEO Howard Schultz had his first cup of coffee? Did Walmart start the day it broke ground on its first mega-store, or the first time Sam Walton realized he could sell more for less? And who's to say where the middle of any business lies?

No, business is much more complicated—yet also quite a bit simpler—than that. In fact, through my various ventures over the years, I've identified not one, not two—not even four or five—but seven phases of business. **The 7 Phases of Business**, which I walk you through in *The Elite Entrepreneur*, are as follows:

- **PHASE 1:** Superior Startup
- **PHASE 2:** Blockbuster Branding
- **PHASE 3:** Sizzling Sales
- **PHASE 4:** Heroic Hiring
- **PHASE 5:** Generating Growth
- **PHASE 6:** Cornering Cash
- **PHASE 7:** Championing Charity

Each section will include relevant anecdotes about business and life, as well as tried-and-true tips, strategies, lists, resources, and steps toward the goal of becoming an Elite Entrepreneur.

You'll learn:

- How to understand the amazing mindset of the Elite Entrepreneur.
- What it takes to have a superior startup.
- How the right brand can generate millions of dollars.
- The powerful yet simple secrets to sales success.
- The importance of hiring the right people at the right time.
- How to "fake it 'til you make it."
- How to generate a cash flow gusher.
- Why social entrepreneurship is the secret to long-range success.

WHAT IS TRUE SUCCESS?

Success is measured in a variety of ways: money, accomplishments, riches, number of employees, popularity of products, homes, cars, satisfaction, and contentment. Anyone can *become* successful (just ask the latest lottery winner), but can they *stay* successful?

If you ever created or built something from scratch and didn't stop until it was finished, you were doing what we entrepreneurs do. We don't even give it a second thought—it's the way our brains work. Part of it is that ability to visualize the end result, hold it in your mind, and keep moving toward your goal. When setbacks come, don't let them beat you down. Just pick up and start over again. Keep navigating your life in that direction and you will reach your goal.

Remember, it's what gets done every day, day in and day out, that makes someone an *Elite Entrepreneur* !

1

BEFORE BEGINNING:

Elite Entrepreneurs Know What They Want

*P*eople who know where they are going are nearly unstoppable. People such as Ray Kroc (McDonald's), Bill Gates (you know who), John Johnson (Ebony), Kemmons Wilson (Holiday Inn), Oprah Winfrey (media mogul), Charles Culpepper (Coca-Cola), and Sam Walton (Walmart) all had a singular vision and the drive to make it happen. Like a bullet, they headed straight for their target.

For Elite Entrepreneurs, the ultimate target is success. It has always been this way. Madam C. J. Walker is listed in *The Guinness Book of World Records* as the first self-made female millionaire in America. This is a noteworthy feat for anyone, but it was particularly so for her because she was the daughter of two freed slaves with little means or education. She didn't accept excuses from anybody, especially herself:

> *"I am a woman who came from the cotton fields of the South. From there I was promoted to the washtub. From there I was promoted to the cook kitchen. And*

> *from there I promoted myself into the business of*
> *manufacturing hair goods and preparations . . . I*
> *have built my own factory on my own ground."*

Examples of success are all around us. Whatever your interests or the career you want to pursue, there are likely others who've forged the way in that field. And if they're still alive, you can probably get in to see them and talk with them. One or two of them could even end up mentoring you.

People who have this kind of single-mindedness about success are bound to achieve their goals. Unfortunately, many entrepreneurs have no direction at all.

I tell them this: "Elite Entrepreneurs know what they want to do."

LACK OF DIRECTION STOPS YOU
BEFORE YOU BEGIN

My suspicion is that people who have no goals and no direction have spent too much time being passive, letting everything happen *to* them. They're used to just getting by. They passively do their job, they passively watch TV, they passively listen to music or watch sports.

They want the easy way to the easy life.

We all need priorities. You need to plan your life

around what is most important to you. Take the time to figure out what you want, what you *really* want, and then make a plan to go for it.

START WITH WHAT YOU KNOW

My best advice is always to do what you love to do. If you do what you love, you'll never feel like you're doing a job. I was just a kid who was crazy about video games. I couldn't get enough of them! In fact, I spent thousands of hours playing those things. As a result, the idea of creating my own video game grew naturally out of something I was already passionate about.

I loved that business. Along the way I found other things I loved doing that I could make money at, too. Once I tasted success being my own boss, I could never work for someone else. Was it work? No way. I enjoyed every minute of the process, and the money I made was just icing on the cake.

WHEN IT'S YOUR PASSION, IT'S NOT WORK!

Before moving to Manhattan, I lived in Kansas, and I remember every day I rode past a cul-de-sac where the kids had set up a ramp and a quarter-pipe so they could skateboard. They were out there every morning before school, practicing hour after hour so they could perfect their flips, turns, and other stunts. I would see them every night when driving home. They were out there, under a streetlight, jumping, flipping, falling, crashing. They sweat and strained and endured endless scrapes, bruises, and cuts in pursuit of mastering the board. When they tried a trick, fell down on the asphalt (hard!), they would get up and try it again. If they got hurt, they'd get a bandage or a cast, wait awhile, and go back to do it again.

These kids put out more physical—and mental—effort in this than they did all day at school. But do you think they considered it work? Of course not. It's what they *lived* for. At the end of the day, their exhaustion and pain were mixed with feelings of satisfaction and inner happiness because they had moved another step closer to achieving a personal goal.

Some of these kids have gone on to become professionals in the sport, others have fine-tuned the equipment, designed their own boards, started their own skateboard parks, traveled around writing about boarding, and on and on. One thing I know for sure: None of them considers all that work as *work*.

It's not a job, it's their passion.

It's no good having material success if you have no passion for the work you do. What kind of enjoyment can come from the drudgery of doing something you don't like, just so you can enjoy some fleeting "lifestyle" moments? That sounds too much like a job to me.

Successful people don't even consider what they do to be work—it's their *passion,* their source of energy, their mission. They get excitement from what they do, and it gives them a great amount of pleasure along the way.

▦

Successful people don't even consider what they do to be work—it's their passion, their source of energy, their mission.

▦

WAKE UP WITH WONDER

Every day I wake up with a head full of plans and ideas. I go to work and meet with people I respect and admire. But most of all, I love the process of taking an idea and making it a reality.

For example, at City Capital we are constantly reviewing proposals from cities to revitalize their urban neighborhoods. Proposals to take rundown areas and turn them into places for new homes and businesses. Or maybe we'll be bring a great historic community back to life and provide affordable homes to working-class families.

Now my newest publicly traded company, Incoming, is embarking on even more exciting ventures, in the emerging field of biofuels. When we closed on the first energy deal, I emailed *The Beverly Hillbillies* theme song to all of my staff around the country. Was any of this *work*? I don't know the meaning of the word! Where there's passion, there is no work. Because every effort is an act of love and generates excitement. Remember that scene in the movie *Back to the Future* where they put garbage in the DeLorean to make it run? We're doing that right now on a prototype scale, and interested cities are already contacting us. Using garbage and other waste products to make diesel and other fuels, and helping people become more self-sufficient and empowered in new ways, have become new passions for me!

WHAT ARE YOU PASSIONATE ABOUT?

To be an Elite Entrepreneur, you don't have to limit yourself to something in which you're currently skilled.

It's more important to have a passion that will drive you. Perhaps you've always admired the way welders can make practically anything out of steel. Even if you've never held a welding torch in your hand, learning how to weld could be a goal you want to pursue.

There are training schools across the country where you can learn not only trades such as welding, but also get leads for dozens of jobs and freelance work. Sure, you'll need to save up money for tuition, but many of those schools have scholarships and student loan programs. So if welding is what you want to do, go for it.

If you can't think of anything you're passionate about, you might need to do some serious "prospecting." By that I mean you might have to look around a bit and find something you think you might enjoy and be able to make money from. What follows is a formula that is familiar and has been used by successful entrepreneurs forever.

FIND A NEED AND FILL IT

All you have to do is look around your neighborhood or your city and think about what people are doing and how you could help them in order to fill a potential need. Are there elderly people in your neighborhood who can't leave the house? Perhaps they need someone who can do their shopping for them.

Are there many single mothers where you live? One of their biggest needs is finding someone who can watch the kids while they go shopping, go to the doctor, or go out with friends. That's a service you could provide. And what about when they go on vacation? You could get paid for staying in their house, eating their food, watching their widescreen TV . . . not too shabby!

One of my first businesses was based on a need that was right in front of me—teenagers without jobs. I knew this because most of my friends were looking for summer jobs. I figured there also had to be some employers and businessmen out there who needed young employees on a part-time or full-time basis. So, being the computer nerd that I was, I knew there had to be a way to use the Internet to match up those employers with those kids looking for work. That's when I got the idea for My First Dot Com Company. The Web site matched kids with jobs, employers with employees. It was a natural fit for me, and a great success as a business.

GO AHEAD, GET CREATIVE!

I love to look around and figure out business opportunities wherever I happen to be. It's this game I play in my mind, to keep myself on the cutting edge. I might drive by a bus stop and see the group of folks waiting. Have you ever had to wait and wait in a doctor's office? Sometimes I wait over an hour. It drives me crazy! People waiting in doctors' offices are a captive audience. What if I installed a video system in those offices with my own programs and advertising? Advertisers might be willing to pay for commercials on that video system. This is the way my mind works—I'm always coming up with ideas. Some of them work out well and some, like the video system, others have developed.

DON'T ASSUME

Let's stop for just a minute, however, and talk about how your idea becomes a business. Many people have a passion for playing the guitar. I see them all the time in parks and on street corners, with a tin can or an old hat to hold tips. That's not the kind of business I'm talking about.

Just like you shouldn't assume your ideas are crazy, you can't automatically assume there is a market for your idea *just because it isn't being done*. That can be just as big a mistake.

For example, I just got back from a speaking tour and ate at a great Serbo-Croatian restaurant. We don't have any of that type of cuisine near where I live. Could be a great opportunity. But just because there *isn't* one in my neighborhood doesn't mean it would be an immediate hit if I opened one.

In fact, there may be very good reasons why there aren't any. It could be that most Americans haven't developed a taste for Serbo-Croatian food yet. Or it could be that the food preparation is too expensive, requiring lots of imported food items whose prices cut into profits. Or perhaps some simple market research might show that only five Serbo-Croatians live within ten miles of me, and that's not nearly enough of an ethnic market to support a startup restaurant.

If you've got an idea for a new product or think you have a way to turn your passion into a business, go for it! But first, do a little research. Ask people if they would buy such a thing. Go online and do some market research on related products, see who leads the field, and find out if there are products that do something similar.

Make a prototype and see if it interests the typical user. In other words, do your due diligence. Some people are so scared they'll get an answer that rejects their idea, they avoid this step. Recognize that as fear, and push through it. You need facts to back up your theory. I learned a concept called "Consumer Driven Information" from a buddy of mine, Fenorris Pearson. Fenorris spent several years at Fortune 500 companies and noticed that company engineers would often create cool "gadgets" that were manufactured but that nobody wanted to buy. So he and his management team began mandating that any inventions be tested on the potential consumers first to see if there was indeed a real market for them. Sounds like common sense, doesn't it? Yet right now across the country there are billions of dollars in inventory sitting in warehouses because ideas were not tested with the consumer first. Fenorris is now an Elite Entrepreneur himself; he is the CEO of Global Consumer Innovation, www.globalconsumerinnovation.com, a high-powered consulting firm that helps individual clients and corporations succeed through new ideas and approaches to business.

Don't fall so in love with your idea or business plan that you become blind to its flaws, or ignore other ways it might work better.

So many business people cling to the "perfect" plan in their mind, unable to see the alternatives that could help it succeed. They doggedly push on, beating against the wall, hoping the wall will move. It doesn't, and, sadly, they fail. And often, they were *that close* . . .

Going from passion to business strategy is a major step. Gathering the information and knowledge you need to succeed will help ensure your success. And being flexible with your idea and strategy will give you the winning edge.

SUPERIOR STARTUP:

*The Owner's Manual for Starting
Your Own Business*

- Elite entrepreneur.
- Startup company.
- On the ground floor.
- Working for myself.

When most of us venture out into the world of entre-preneurism, these are the phrases we think of most. We have been taught to visualize the trappings of our success—things like the size of our office, the number of employees, the packaging of our products, and the size of our bank accounts.

What we have not been taught is to visualize the challenges we might face, such as the transparency of social media, the legal requirements, the financial requirements related to having employees and office space, and, of course, details like handicapped parking. It's obviously much more fun to imagine your first-quarter earnings check rather than your legal bills, but we must picture both income *and* expenses, because unfortunately you can't have one without the other.

In this country there's this business fantasy world that says, "Hey, I'm going to come up with this idea. I'm going to write an eighty-page business plan, people are going give me tons of money, and I'm going to be the next Google or Facebook."

Well, Elite Entrepreneurs don't buy into that fantasy. Instead, they create Superior Startups.

WHAT IS A SUPERIOR STARTUP?

Before we get to what a Superior Startup is, let's talk about the two things a Superior Startup *isn't*:

1. **A suite of fancy offices before the first dollar is made.** Startups aren't superior because they look good, they're superior because they *are* good. They have good plans, good goals, and good people who work well together.

2. **An idea with no substance.** The foundation of a Superior Startup is a principal idea around which everything else is built. In a Superior Startup, the idea comes first, not the logo, the brand name, or the home office address.

So, if that's what a Superior Startup isn't . . . what *is* it? A Superior Startup is one that does things the right way, in the right order, for the right reasons. A Superior Startup recognizes that money is always limited, and that the money needs to go to the people and the products/ services first. The fancy office furniture, high-tech phone lines, and receptionist come second.

In this chapter I'm going to teach you exactly how to have that image of the classy, organized, thoughtful startup, without blowing through cash to get it. Instead, I'll help you put the money where it really needs to be and show you how to use limited resources to launch your company, keep it intact, and keep your sanity as you go.

I'll also show you how to set up your company from the beginning to be scalable, deployable, and growth-oriented, while building it with an eye to being sold or acquired.

DON'T BE ON A PROFESSIONAL SUICIDE MISSION: How to Enter and Exit in the Same Business Plan

What makes my approach to starting a business different from the thousands of other approaches found in books and magazines, online, or at seminars, classes, etc.? Well, my approach goes completely against the grain of those thousands of others.

First of all, they tell you to write a business plan. Now, if you talked to me and my other entrepreneur buddies, you'd know very few of us have ever raised money off of a business plan. And here's why: I've been an investment banker. I know how money works, how it flows, how it gets borrowed, and how it gets lent. So, do investment bankers read business plans? No! At least not in the beginning.

In fact, one of the key things most bankers look for when asked to raise capital for any venture is the exit strategy. A lot of people will tell you, "Hey, go start your company of your dreams, build it up, and figure out the exit strategy later." No, you figure out the exit strategy and where you want to be first, then you start building the plan around exactly how you're going to get there.

What's striking to me, as both an entrepreneur and a former investment banker, is that there are so many entrepreneurs who start businesses without any exit strategy at all. Who is advising them on this strategy? It certainly isn't bankers; it certainly isn't an Elite Entrepreneur.

Being an Elite Entrepreneur is just like being a well-trained combat soldier. You don't go into a mission unless you know how you're going to get out of the firefight. But so many people who read and follow entrepreneurial how-to books are being dropped into the firefight as if on a suicide mission.

So that's one of the essentials of creating a Superior Startup: Know going in how you're going to get out!

IT'S ALL ABOUT THE BENJAMINS:
Money and Other Challenges You Will Face
as an Elite Entrepreneur

People ask me all the time, "Ephren, what are some of the most common challenges an entrepreneur will face during the startup phase?" That's a little like asking someone, "What's the hardest part about being married?" or "What challenges did you face after your first baby?"

Everyone has a different answer. For me, however, there are only three: money, money, and money. Did I mention money? Okay, actually I'm exaggerating (kind of). Here are the biggest challenges facing nearly every entrepreneur, and particularly Elite Entrepreneurs:

■ **CHALLENGE NUMBER 1:** *Money, Money, Money*

One of the most common challenges entrepreneurs face during the startup phase is the acquisition of capital. We will devote several sections to acquiring capital throughout this book, but it is important to know going in that money is the driving force behind all startup organizations: getting it, making it, keeping it, and leaving with some—hopefully you're walking away with millions—as part of your exit strategy.

You don't have to be a financial wizard to be an Elite Entrepreneur, but if you're not, know that you're not and get help. Find a mentor, get an accountant, read a book, get advice. Whenever, wherever. Ideas are what make entrepreneurs go into business, but it's money that makes ideas a reality.

▪ CHALLENGE NUMBER 2: *Forming the Right Team*

You can't do it all alone.

That is my message to countless entrepreneurs all over the country, and it's something I learned the hard way. It may be your idea that starts the company, it may be your passion that rallies the troops, but without troops to rally, your idea will never reach its potential.

It is so important to have the right people around you when you're taking that company to the next level. True, you can perform a lot of the groundwork on your own, but when it comes time to make your plans a reality, people will always be your most valuable resource.

In the past, I built many companies through blood, sweat, and tears, but because I was doing most of the work myself, I started well behind my competition. But once I learned the importance of people—valuable team players—I was able to catch up to and even pass my competitors. When you get the right people, you can make things happen in as little as a week, while companies working with no people, or the wrong people, will take months or more—if at all.

■ **CHALLENGE NUMBER 3:** *Personal and Brand Identity— Finding the Laser Focus*

Something else I stress all the time to entrepreneurs is how important it is to try to define exactly who in the world they are. I've seen a ton of entrepreneurs who have fifty million great ideas, and they're putting them all out there, one Web site, product, or service after another. But there's really no identity.

There's no identity for the actual business; they're missing what I call a "laser focus" around the personal brand. Richard Branson, for example, has his hands in everything: music, jets, retail, fashion, cell phones. Yet even though he cross-promotes across a variety of different industries, people trust his *personal* brand, so the message doesn't get diluted.

It's the same thing with Magic Johnson. This former-basketball-great-turned-business titan is involved in commercial real estate, movie theaters, writing books, community development, and, above all, encouraging young entrepreneurs. But the "Magic Johnson" brand is so laser-focused and pronounced, people trust that brand more than many others. My management team at Ascendant Strategy refers to this as the "CEO brand." Let's be candid, are Branson and Johnson successful simply because they come up with good ideas? Absolutely not—many people come up with great ideas. What Branson and Johnson have is a *CEO brand* that is recognizable and that people want to be associated with. People believe in those brands and associate success with them.

So how do you get that laser focus for your own entrepreneurial brand, whether you have one product or a hundred? Getting that laser focus is a discipline that has to be learned. And Elite Entrepreneurs realize that focus can be a gift and a curse; they can see a lot of things that other people can't see.

For example, if you point that laser focus in one direction, you have the power to move mountains, but if you wave it willy-nilly, scattered across a variety of projects—without mastering it first—you're going to fracture the personal brand and people will feel you're "all over the place." It's okay to have dozens of ideas and even several companies, but in all things you do, you must learn to focus your energies around not just the product or service of the moment, but on how they fit with your personal brand as an Elite Entrepreneur. What do those products or services say about you? How do they add to your existing product or service lines? What will they take away from them, or add to them?

It's a discipline you will need to be able to control. It's like Cyclops from the X-Men. If he takes those glasses off, that laser ray just goes everywhere and he can't control it. But when he puts those glasses back on, then he can focus his laser ray on the exact spot and do some real damage.

Once you master that laser focus, you, too, can go from being an entrepreneur who's all over the place to one who's a business superhero with a vision—or what I call an Elite Entrepreneur. So, getting that laser focus means going through a series of disciplines. It means reading the right materials and books, taking classes, and learning the ropes. But it also means surrounding yourself with other very focused people.

Every elite talent needs a mentor, a role model, a sage. Cyclops had Professor X of the X-Men to guide and nurture him and, from time to time, to pull in the reins. It took me a long time to realize I sometimes needed to be pulled back. Having a professional mentor helped me professionally. When I first met Wendy Connor, she had already successfully built and sold companies for ten figures. I asked her to come in as chief operating officer of City Capital, and for the first six months she put me on a "time-out" in my own company. It was a reality check that showed me just because you developed the battle plan doesn't mean you're the best soldier. Wendy mentored me even though "technically" I was her supervisor.

WITH AGE COMES WISDOM

Ten years ago my entrepreneurial philosophy was, "Hey, great idea, let's stay up all night and on the weekends. Let's build it and go from there." But what I quickly discovered was that when you start a company without having the endgame in mind, you always have to go back and do it all over again.

It's a little like writing a murder mystery without knowing who the killer is at the end. You're going to have to go back to the beginning of the story and rewrite the clues to fit whoever winds up being the guilty party. Know the ending before you begin.

I approach things a little differently now; I move a little bit slower, and I'm very deliberate. In addition to plotting the endgame at the beginning, I will always **put the right people around the project first.**

Now, the minute I get an idea, I bounce it off all my experts, my advisory board (more on that later), my council, and everybody else I know to get the feedback, to predict the potential potholes. Then I'll find an industry expert who's done it, been there, and made it happen. Then I will recruit that person onto the team to do the same thing: check for potholes, get feedback, etc.

For example, we're looking at launching a multilevel

marketing company, something I don't have a ton of personal experience in. So rather than rushing in full-speed ahead and going back to "do the rewrites" later, this time I made sure to figure out the ending first. So we brought in people who have already launched twenty to thirty multilevel marketing companies and picked their brains, gave them jobs on the board, made them our focus group and our advisory board. Today I feel confident moving forward.

CONSTANT SOLUTIONS TO EVERYDAY CHALLENGES

Creating a Superior Startup, to say nothing of being an Elite Entrepreneur, means facing challenges on an almost daily basis. Some of those challenges are lightweight, others are heavyweights, but all can be met—and overcome—if you have a system in place for addressing current challenges and avoiding future ones.

For example, we recently faced a challenge around the pricing of a certain service we were offering. Now, trying to determine how much you should charge may seem like a pretty minor challenge, but it is, in fact, difficult and something that we face in every one of our businesses.

One of the products we're currently selling was doing well, but not well enough; it was successful, but I felt it could become more successful. It was getting out there, but we still weren't making enough money on it. We were debating what is a common issue to most entrepreneurs: Do we lower the price to get more volume, or do we increase the price and hopefully earn more revenue? And so me being me, I decided to lower the price. Big mistake!

We lowered the price and sales tanked. It made absolutely no sense. We were selling plenty at one price point and then we lowered it by almost half and sales tanked immediately. We sold less and made way less money for almost a month. We were almost broke. Then one of my advisors said, "I believe we're offering a premium service, so let's raise the price." And I said, "Look, it didn't work with lowering the price. What makes you think it's going to work higher?" But, on a whim, he said, "Trust me on this."

We raised the price, and we shattered records. Nothing changed except the price; it was the exact same product, the exact same offer, just at a different—and may I point out, *higher*—price. Yet for some reason, sales shot through the roof.

So, I'll make the point again: To reduce some challenges and overcome others, you *have* to get the right people around you. You have to have the right information being fed to you. It's important to see the problem from all angles. In this situation, if it had been just me alone in my office staring out the window, I would have kept lowering the price or given up entirely. But with the proper advice I was able to not only salvage the situation, but to make it profitable—very profitable.

That said, advice is just that—advice. At the end of the day, as the person in charge, you must be prepared to sometimes go against the grain of conventional thought. And when you do, you'll be amazed at the things that can happen.

As the person in charge, you must be prepared to sometimes go against the grain of conventional thought. And when you do, you'll be amazed at the things that can happen.

For example, about a year ago, we started a mentorship group, and it was soon growing fast. We had aligned with a group that was supposed to come in and bring thousands of subscribers, but all of a sudden the agency that was overseeing it said, "No, you guys can't do this."

So, after enrolling a couple hundred people, we had

to purge the whole system of all those users and start over. Our new company went from making $30,000 a month to $30 a month. We kept thinking, what in the world are we going to do? Our major challenge was to draw in a mass of people without the assistance of that one main client.

Many traditional entrepreneurs have that one great idea, that one thing they're pursuing, but if it falls through, they're suddenly asking themselves, "What do we do now? We're ruined!" But in our situation with the mentoring project, I decided not to sit around waiting for something to happen, but to find ways to *make* something happen.

We bounced an idea off of our network, and in whirlwind fashion—and I mean within forty-eight hours quick—we threw something together. We decided to shoot for the moon because we had nothing to lose. So we went out, put it in place, and over the course of six weeks, we signed up almost four thousand people for this new product and service that people said couldn't work.

So when your back is against the wall and you're losing money, or your one big client falls through, or an opportunity or big sale doesn't pan out, you can't give up. You have to try something new. You have to be bold; you have to be innovative.

IF YOU HAVE TO FAIL, YOU MIGHT AS WELL FAIL WELL

Failure is one of those things most of us would prefer to avoid altogether. Unfortunately, failure is a part of life, and no matter how successful you are, it's just as easy to fail as it is to succeed.

Consider the story of James Cameron, who despite having created *Titanic,* the number one blockbuster of all time, was still eager to put another big, game-changing story on the big screen. The result was *Avatar,* a movie many of his critics felt would fail so miserably it would end his career. The result was quite the opposite, however; *Avatar* is now ranked as the highest-grossing movie of all time and is certainly one of Cameron's biggest professional triumphs. When asked by a CNN reporter about fearing failure, Cameron had this to say: "In whatever you're doing, failure is an option, but fear is not."

I agree. You have to be willing to fail in order to succeed and, in fact, you *will* fail more times than you succeed. I know I have, as has nearly every entrepreneur to whom I've ever spoken.

Now, there are a couple of ways you can fail. One, you can just flat-out fail miserably, and say, "Oh, woe is me." You just quit and go home and cry like a baby. (Been there, done that.) The other type of failure is the type of guy who falls down, gets back up, re-evaluates, looks around, and tries to figure out how not to fall down again. How do I not trip over this rock? Do I need to jump earlier? Do I need to jump later? Do I not jump at all?

That is an Elite Entrepreneur. They will fail well. They will fall down, and in doing so, figure out the way to fall correctly next time, just like stunt people in the movies do (yep, there's a proper way to get hit by a car, to tuck and roll to avoid getting hurt). Learning the techniques of how to fail allows you to get up quickly, recover, and reassess. Failure is a teachable moment.

Failure is also an opportunity. Or, as Ralph Waldo Emerson said, "Every wall is an opportunity." So many entrepreneurs fail and give up, and you know when they give up? Unfortunately, it's often just before the economy gets better, or the stock market gets better, or real estate gets better, or a market opens up for their product.

In my life, I've had a number of companies just not work and actually fail. Did we give up? No, we went back to the drawing board. We had our debriefing to figure out what worked and what didn't, and applied those particular lessons. We went back out and tried it again and again and again. And with the persistence of an Elite Entrepreneur, you can make anything happen when you fail well.

Persistence is the key to success, and the key to persistence is failing well.

SUPERIOR STARTUP—8 STEPS FOR STARTING A BUSINESS

So, we've covered the challenges to creating a Superior Startup, and learned there are many. The good news, though, is that I have devised a simple, eight-step system that will help you not only handle the challenges that do arise, but help prevent them from appearing in the first place.

- **STEP 1:** *Define What the Business Will Be*

Remember what I said earlier about having a laser focus? That applies here as well. The first step, before raising one single dollar, before finding one single mentor, before developing one single product, is to have one single driving idea around which the company will be centered.

The beauty of our modern times is that almost anything can succeed these days. From personalized gardening tools to flavored peanut butter to gourmet barbecue sauces to video games to financial services to new machinery lubricant, nearly every idea, in every industry, is fair game.

No idea is out of bounds; and I mean none. Who in the world thought there would ever be enough interest in fancy soaps and bubble bath to build a worldwide company around? Well, the folks at Bath & Body Works did. Whoever thought folks would love coffee enough to support thousands of coffee shops all over the world? Well, the folks behind Starbucks did.

The point is, no company can succeed without a single, driving vision. It's more than a mission statement; it's the actual mission. What is your mission? To succeed? How are you going to succeed? By building a company. What are you going to build your company around?

That is the question you, and you alone, can answer. So, define what the business will be. Write it down in a single sentence. Why just a single sentence? **Because if you can't tell people what your product or service is in one sentence, your vision is not a clear enough and your laser focus is decidedly unfocused.**

Here, I'll get you started. The first step to building a Superior Startup is to finish this simple sentence:

"I am going to build a business that will

_____

_____ ."

■ **STEP 2:** *Create a One-Sheet*

From one sentence we move to one sheet of paper; I call it the "one-sheet," and it's Step 2 of this Superior Startup process. The one-sheet contains the exact, precise details about how you're going to structure this company. It identifies who your partners are, who's going to be working with you, how you're going to put the money in and where it's going to come from. And the best part is, you have to condense all this information on to one sheet of paper.

Yes, it sounds like madness. Yes, it sounds like it's going to be a mighty small font, but put it all on one piece of paper. If you can't articulate it in one piece of paper, you already have a problem.

Companies that start out complicated don't get simpler; they just get more complicated. Companies that start out simply only get simpler because they begin with a philosophy of "less is more," and that philosophy continues through everything they do from that point out.

All of my companies, no matter how big or how small, have started with a simple sheet of paper that included the following:

- Company name
- Company mission (see Step 1, above)
- Company leaders

- Company financier(s)
- Company structure
- Company start date
- Company exit plan

■ STEP 3: *Research Your Competitors and Your Industry*

You should start by doing a lot of research on who your competitors are, what they're charging, what consumers think of them, and whether you can come up with a viable way to be the "anti" to them.

For example, a few years ago the pizza delivery market was pretty crowded because Domino's and Pizza Hut had it locked up. But then an upstart competitor thought he could be the "anti" pizza delivery company—enter Papa John's. John Schnatter founded Papa John's in 1984 from the back of a bar he owned with his dad. Today there are 3,000 Papa John's franchises, and he is a force to be reckoned with for industry dominators Domino's and Pizza Hut. How did he do it? Clearly, Schnatter saw the two dominant pizza chains as impersonal corporations, companies with no recognizable face, leader, or even a personality, as far as the buying public was concerned. Like Coke and Pepsi, they were two similar companies; people either preferred Pizza Hut or Domino's and that was that.

But Schnatter clearly recognized that if he gave customers an alternative—a name and a face—they could recognize and relate to, it might just pay off. And did it ever! If you look at a Domino's or Pizza Hut Web site, you see pizzas, breadsticks, or wings; if you look at Papa John's Web site, you see . . . John Schnatter. Even the ads feature the founder, often in the kitchen cooking up pizzas or, more recently, personally delivering pizzas to his customers. Clearly, he analyzed the competition and found a place to fit.

So should you.

Next, determine what the industry is like. Is the industry big enough? Is somebody already running with your idea? If there's somebody in that field and they're being successful, then what is it that makes them successful? When we were considering our iPhone application, we did a couple of case studies. We did some test groups. We were bouncing ideas off family, friends, industry experts, anyone and everyone we could. Then on top of that, we enlisted everybody and their moms to surf the Internet, looking at different applications, their features, their price points. We talked to different ad agencies, and it didn't cost us a dime. We were just making phone calls and asking, "Hey, what do you think about this as an idea?" And then we started putting our partners together and interviewing the various developers, getting rates and schedules.

We had our budget in place. We had our costs. We had our timeline. Why? Because we did our research first. So we'd broken it down to a project plan, mapping how we were going to launch the company, put it together, put the right legal structure in place for its particular partners, determine how it was going to be capitalized, and the money needed to do so.

And then on top of that, by leveraging our resources, we spent far less than anybody else in our category because we did the research and intelligence gathering on the front end. We also saved ourselves a ton of time and actually get to market sooner because of the groundwork we'd already laid.

■ **STEP 4:** *Match the Players with the Team*

In a Superior Startup, you're the coach. Who do you coach? The team. Who's on the team? Ah, there's the key to Step 4: Match the Players with the Team. Every organization needs certain key players: your money people, your creative people, your legal people, your human resources people, your product development people.

Your people have to work together, and the partnership tone you set from day one needs to be a tone that sticks. If marketing doesn't get along with sales, then you're going to have a problem. If sales doesn't get along with product development, then you're going to have two problems. When it comes to teams, the more problems you have, the less success you achieve.

The great thing is you're just starting out, so you get to handpick the team. Like your laser focus, that can be a blessing and a curse. Put together the right team, and the journey to success is a whole lot easier. Pick the wrong team, and you could be signing your company's death sentence.

Take your time with this step; it's too important to rush. Don't just hire individuals, hire team players. See how they work together. One thing I like to do as I'm putting together my team is to spend a lot of time with them.

Hold retreats, board meetings, focus groups, and brainstorm sessions; have lunches and dinners together. See how everyone interacts. You will quickly see who fits —and who doesn't. Don't be afraid to get rid of the sore thumbs who stick out; they'll only poke you in the eye later if you hang onto them.

- **STEP 5:** *Legalize It*

Now that you have the structure together, you break out the lawyers. You have them legalize it, type it all up. If you don't have a lawyer, that means you have to do some do-it-yourself legal research. It means that you'll have to go to your local bookstore and pick up some books, and/or go online and download some forms. For fast startup help, I know several people who have used bizfilings.com. I must caution you, however, about setting the legal stuff up yourself.

If at all possible, try to find a lawyer you can work with, someone who can be a business partner. My attorney, Robert Bovarnick (www.bovarnickandassociates.com), is a good example. I pay him hundreds of thousands of dollars a year, but he saves me *millions*. Obviously, you get what you pay for in the legal profession. Cheap attorneys mean cheap results. One strategy is to offer equity in exchange for services, which allows you to get the good legal representation without paying the huge upfront fees that tie up your cash flow. That may sound almost impossible, but start talking to lawyer after lawyer after lawyer until you can find one who will be able to help you. I need to put in this disclaimer: Hire your attorney upfront, as close to the beginning of your venture as possible. If you wait too long, you will have to pay much more to clean up the legal mess you've already created. That is a lesson I learned the hard way.

There are many big law firms out there that would love to take positions or a piece of action in the next great startup or business. Specifically, there are law firms where that's all they do. But once again, it comes back to leveraging your network. Ask your mentors, your friends, and your colleagues what attorneys and firms they've used in the past. Then try them on for size yourself.

■ STEP 6: *Form a Mentor Advisory Board*

It's critical that as you begin to frame out your Superior Startup, you form what I call a Mentor Advisory Board. You need guardrails for your great ideas, for your enthusiasm, for your creativity; these are the people that provide them.

You will find mentors in every industry, in every walk of life, in every church, in every corner you come to. Pick the right ones for YOU. Mentors, like every other team member, should get along with the group; they should "fit" with you and your personal and professional needs.

That doesn't mean they will always agree with you; in fact, you want mentors to play the "devil's advocate" role, disagreeing with you, if only to get you to see an opportunity or challenge—or even failure—from a different perspective.

That's why it's critical to have a legal expert devise roles for each member of your team determine how each is going to participate. You can't always afford to pay your Mentor Advisory Board, but they're critical to your success, so you'll want to offer them some sort of incentive to get them on board.

Once they are, mine these sages for every piece of advice they can offer. Before you launch a new product or develop your company logo—or even your company business cards—discuss it with your Mentor Advisory Board.

Trust me, you'll be glad you did.

■ STEP 7: *Develop Your Launch Plan*

The launch plan is critical and one of your final steps before "going live." I consider the launch plan a dress rehearsal, putting everything down and seeing how it will work out on paper and, as often as possible, in real life.

Here's the thing about the launch plan; it's not just about your launch. It's about a week after your launch, a month after your launch, even a year after your launch— and then some.

What's a launch plan look like? When I do one, I make it out like a playbook, where all team members know what their roles and responsibilities are. For example, marketing should know what they need to do by launch date, by the first week after launch, by first month after, etc.

Be very detailed here; list job requirements, deadlines, deliverables, and anything and everything you need to hold folks accountable. Do this for *every* department. Then do it for yourself.

I know it sounds like a work, especially since you're doing this on top of a lot of *other* work. But you really do have to have these details in place so everybody knows where they're supposed to be at what particular time. It's like creating a playbook where everyone truly believes your plays will work. Why? Because all of them know exactly what they have to do, and when.

It's not a business plan; it's an action plan. Action plans matter. Business plans are nothing more than plans. Action means this is what we're going to do, when we're going to do it, and how we're going to do it.

■ **STEP 8:** *Never Stop Raising Money*

Finally, let's talk money. You need it. You need it now, you'll need it tomorrow, you'll need it the day after tomorrow and a month and a year after tomorrow. Money is one of the constant headaches—and perks— of being the Elite Entrepreneur.

Never assume you have enough money. Never get lazy and quit networking with potential investors and financiers. Keep good relations with your bank(s); talk to them often. Have your finance people always looking for better rates and better programs. Have a point person at your bank and talk to him or her frequently. Let that person know about your business and how it works; they can be on the lookout for new ways to help you.

Be looking for ways to save money. **Never forget that saving money is the same as making money!**

Don't assume your cleaning people, package deliverer, or water cooler guys are giving you the best deal; talk to them and make sure. Have someone on staff devoted to shaving expenses when, how, and if they can; this will pay off in ways that will amaze you.

Now, if you're looking for me to be your coach, as somebody who's been there and done that, go to www.eliteephren.com, where I show entrepreneurs like you the challenges and successes we go through and then offer step-by-step instructions on how you can put it all in place. Because there's not enough space in these pages to cover all of the details, my online mastery programs are great forums where you can learn from other mentors and coaches of mine, and get a plethora of information to help you along on your entrepreneurial journey.

If you go to Ephren Taylor's Elite Entrepreneur program (www.eliteephren.com), I'll provide you with my top twenty-five resources for getting your business off the ground quickly and efficiently, as well as some templates you can use that accompany this book and will help you start putting that action plan together.

PLAN YOUR GREAT ESCAPE: Or, What Makes an Unsuccessful Startup?

If you were locked in prison for the rest of your life, would you simply give up and stay confined, or would you try to break out? I think most of us would work night and day to find a way out of that prison cell. Well, working in a job you can't stand, always being in debt, not living up to your full potential—these are the prison cells we lock ourselves in each day.

A Superior Startup is like that big prison break; you don't just rush into it—you plan first. You scout out the area; you case the joint. What time do the guards come by? When is the security alarm going to be down for maintenance? Sure, you can think about it every day but don't pull the trigger until you're good and ready or you'll wind up in solitary confinement!

So you'd get a crew together, a crew of people you could trust, and every day, and every night, this crew would talk about nothing but your big escape. You'd want your crew to be experts, the best in their fields, folks who have done this before. Even if this is your first startup, you can't have a team full of first-timers or you'll dig that escape tunnel right under the guard tower.

So you need a few experts, some mentors, to put guardrails on your creativity to make sure you get where you need to go, even if it isn't exactly the way you've always pictured it. If you don't take these steps, you're going to miss out on your big break. You'll not only be stuck in that mental prison, you'll be what I consider an unsuccessful startup. Just what is an unsuccessful startup? It's a startup that never starts. It just ends in conversation over and over again. Have you ever met somebody who talks about an idea, or what he's going to do, or what should happen, but never does anything about it? That's an unsuccessful startup.

Elite Entrepreneurs talk plenty—my network is constantly mouthing off—but they back it up. They put together those action plans I talk about and start assembling a team that is going to make it a success. Then through pushing, screaming, pulling, they do whatever it takes to get it done.

BLOCKBUSTER BRANDING:

The Master Plan for Branding Your New Business

$\mathcal{M}$any companies consider branding synonymous with marketing and PR, but **branding is about creating an identity that is recognizable as yours—** and yours alone. More important, because we're all here to make money, it's about creating a brand that can be monetized. You may think you have a great brand, but if it's not appealing to customers, if it doesn't make them reach for their wallets, how great can it really be?

A brand is a living thing, something that exists over and above and outside and beyond the things you do to create it. You work long and hard on your brand and then you send it out into the world, and that is where its strength determines whether it lives or dies.

In this chapter I am going to talk not just about branding but about something I call Blockbuster Branding, the new and modern way of branding yourself in today's pop culture by using research, creative teams, and social media to create a brand that truly gets people talking.

WHAT GIVES "BLOCKBUSTER"
BRANDING BLOCKBUSTER STATUS?

Why do I call it "Blockbuster" Branding? Simple: Some movies are blockbusters, while others just kind of come out flat, doing okay business but not really getting the audience buzzing.

What makes one movie a blockbuster and another a solid performer? That's a mystery Hollywood has been trying to figure out for years, but it's you and I and everyone else who buys a ticket that makes a so-so movie a blockbuster.

And it often has very little to do with the movie itself. Savvy filmmakers know that to turn a regular movie into a blockbuster movie, they need to do something to brand that movie in the audience's mind—long before the movie even comes out.

So they make a cool trailer and preview it with other blockbuster movies months in advance. Or they may float some big rumor online that makes people interested in the movie, or publicize a controversial scene—anything to create interest and entice people to see that movie.

For example, Twentieth Century Fox recently issued a press release saying *Die Hard 5* would feature the character Jack Bauer (played by Kiefer Sutherland) from the hit show *24*. By any standard, such an announcement would create immediate buzz and generate interest from the loyal viewers of *24*, a show that received Emmy nominations each year it was on the air. The release went on to say that Kiefer Sutherland ended up dismissing the idea, but the producers of *Die Hard 5* would be including elements of the global terror storyline in the movie. On the surface it doesn't make much sense to create buzz about a something that *isn't* going to happen, but Twentieth Century Fox knew *exactly* what it was doing.

It's more than just "buzz," because buzz can quickly die if it's not properly maintained before, during, and after a movie comes out. It's genuine interest, something people are talking about. And the more people talk about it, the more other people are determined to "see what everybody is talking about." And seeing what everybody is talking about is the strength from which blockbusters are made.

If the *Die Hard* producers had simply put out a release saying *Die Hard 5* was going to include a global terror storyline, it wouldn't have piqued much interest and perhaps would have gotten criticism from the series fans who like the more local storylines of the previous films. But by leveraging *24* and Jack Bauer, the announcement piques new interest and gets people's minds spinning. They wonder how Twentieth Century Fox will pull off this fifth film. At the time of this book's publication, the movie isn't due out for nearly two years!

Even before the movie is released, people are anticipating it; once the movie comes out, people are talking about it. And as you'll soon discover, **branding is simply a way to get people talking about your product or a service.** The same way audience Word of Mouth drives people either to or from a movie, it will drive people to or from your company brand.

This chapter is designed to make your brand more than just a brand; it's designed to make it a Blockbuster Brand.

ADS ARE WHAT THEY *SEE*; BRANDS ARE WHAT THEY *SAY*

I always say that *marketing* is what people *see about you*—commercials, print ads, blog posts, Web banner ads, chats and social media, billboards—and *branding* is what people *say about you*. Because when you have a solid brand, one with a proven identity, it's something people talk about long after the commercial is over or they've driven by that giant billboard.

A successful brand is something that you put out into the world—a mood or a theme or a thought or an attitude—and it just lives there, growing and multiplying on its own. That's the beauty of a brand, particularly a

Blockbuster Brand. It's not marketing and it's not PR, because those things cost you money. Once you've built a brand, it lives on in perpetuity because it has a life of its own.

I'm not saying that once a successful brand is established you won't still have to market and do PR. You do. Do you think Pepsi or Nike or Apple will ever stop advertising? Heck no. But in addition to that advertising, they have the benefit of a proven brand, meaning they don't have to advertise as much, meaning there's more money in their pockets because they're spending less on marketing and PR and letting customers like you and me do the work.

THE BLOCKBUSTER BRAND TEST

Here are some Blockbuster Brands you and I know and love. In the left-hand column I've put the name of the brand, and next to it I've put two blanks. In the blanks below each brand, I'd like you to put the first two words that come to mind when you see the brand name.

Don't think about it, don't mull it over, don't consider what's politically correct or what I might think of those two words or what the guy reading over your shoulder in the bookstore might think. Just put the first two words that come to your mind.

- Bed, Bath & Beyond

_____   _____

- Sprite

_____   _____

- Ritz Crackers

_____   _____

- Nike

_____   _____

- Bath & Body Works

_____   _____

- McDonald's

_____   _____

Now here is that list again with *my* two words next to each brand:

- Bed, Bath & Beyond   *variety*   *quality*

- Sprite   *refreshing*   *youthful*

- Ritz Crackers   *tasty*   *entertaining*

- Nike   *athletic*   *quality*

- Bath & Body Works   *clean*   *fragrant*

- McDonald's   *convenient*   *affordable*

Did we match up? I've given the Blockbuster Brand Test in countless seminars, and sometimes folks use the exact same words for each brand as I did, and sometimes they use variants of the same words. Most of us think of words like "athletic" and "quality" and "status" and "excellence" and "athletes" when we see the word Nike and "refreshing" and "cold" and "young" and "clean" when we see the word Sprite.

This is what I mean by the work customers do on your behalf. All Sprite and Nike and McDonald's and Bed, Bath & Beyond have to do is build a brand—a strong, recognizable, successful brand—and half their work is done for them.

LONGEVITY AND MONETIZATION:
The Twin Pillars of a Successful Brand

A successful brand is one that when people mention it in conjunction with your company name, it becomes synonymous with pop culture. And if you can create a campaign with ties to pop culture, if you can create a campaign that's synonymous with culture or analogous to it, you've created something that has longevity and can be monetized.

Longevity and *monetization* are two attributes we've been working on for years with our branding firm, Ascendant Strategy (www.ascendantstrategy.net). Longevity means you make decisions that aren't just good in the short-term, but that make sense in the long-term as well.

Ascendant doesn't work with every client who walks through the door. It is important to work with companies that are specialized and not firms that take in anybody and everybody. The firms that horde clients tend to bring less specific strategies to the table, and if you're going to win in business you need to be differentiated, unique.

So we don't blitz thousands of colleges and corporations looking for just any speaking gig. Instead, we consistently try to focus on quality organizations that will help us put on dependable seminars on topics of interest in that particular market.

Personalization is the key to branding yourself well, so every customer gets that personal attention and remembers you not just as a company, but as *people* working at a company.

Recently I started a publicly traded brand-acceleration firm, Incoming, Inc. Incoming takes brands with great potential, puts additional investment and strategy behind them to accelerate the brand's success, and monetize the brand. I can't emphasize brand monetization enough. If you're in business, you're not building a brand to be cool; you're building it and leveraging it with accelerated and sustainable monetization as the ultimate goal. In other words, you want it to make money.

I work just as hard on my PR branding as I do on my financial investing branding. And now when people think about socially responsible investing, what in the world comes up? My company City Capital Corporation and, by association, my name, Ephren Taylor. City Capital is considered one of the most socially responsible companies in the world. One of my speaking topics is "corporate social responsibility." Do you get the connection? If you want your company to be known for something and you want to turn it in a certain direction, as the chief messaging officer you have to be on message all the time and continually remind your team what that message is. It would have been much more difficult for City Capital to make this claim if I hadn't been constantly talking about corporate social responsibility on national TV shows and during speeches across the globe.

So I want to help entrepreneurs like you create these brand and blockbuster capabilities but also show you some of the economic benefits of creating a brand versus simply having a solid marketing plan.

And believe me, there's a *huge* difference.

YOUR BRAND IS THE ESSENCE OF YOUR COMPANY

I think one of the first things you need to do when it comes to building your brand is to stop thinking of it as something different and apart from what you do on a daily basis.

A brand is not what you do; it's who you are.

When I hear people talking about branding, they usually do it synonymously with some already-famous brand, such as Coke or Pepsi, Microsoft or Apple, McDonald's or Burger King. As if just because they start "branding," consumers will magically start associating their products with "youth" or "athletic" or "excellence" or "convenience" or "refreshment."

But you can't act like an old company and brand yourself as youthful; you can't just phone it in and convey excellence. Companies like Coca-Cola, Nike, and Amazon and Apple have excellent brands because they are excellent companies.

They understand that they don't just promote their company, they promote their brand. Transparency is one of the modern benefits of social media and a 24/7/365 newsfeed.

As a result, almost all of us have seen some of the inner workings of corporations like Nike and McDonald's, and what we see in the factories, the corporate offices, the test kitchens, and the commercials is synergistic.

In other words, what Nike does in its corporate offices, down to the last stapler and cubicle, is reflected in its brand: They hire youthful, energetic, athletic people to tout a brand that is youthful, energetic, and athletic.

At McDonald's Hamburger University, they don't just train new employees how to flip burgers or squirt ketchup, but to live the McDonald's brand of fast, hot, convenient, and affordable food.

Southwest Airlines focuses on being the low-cost airline. Every decision Southwest people make, from whether or not to offer food, whether or not passengers should pay for luggage, or whether or not flights would show movies, is run through the brand paradigm. If an action helps Southwest's brand as the low-cost airline, they will do it. If not, they don't. Simple, yet it takes an incredible amount of discipline to make sure their internal decision-making processes help them stay true to their brand.

So when you think brand, don't just think billboards and banner ads—those are advertisements. They're for the multimillion-dollar companies, not for startups (unless you were given an eight-figure seed capital deal). I have an attorney friend, let's call him Peter, who has a successful law firm that does nearly two million in revenue a year, and he's gotten much of his business through traditional billboard advertising, radio spots, and TV commercials in two markets. While Peter is excited about these results, and I do commend him, I look at Peter sometimes and want to shake him because he isn't being an Elite Entrepreneur. If Peter focused on branding, his conversion rate for all those billboard, radio, and TV ads would be much higher simply because his name would "stick" more.

Branding isn't a billboard, branding is the bat signal! You know the bat signal, this big bat-shaped beacon that gets shined into the night to summon Batman. It means the authorities need help, and when they turn on that bat signal, they'll get the help they need. That is what your brand is like—a big, shining beacon calling customers to you. If customers have pain or a need, when they think of you, they know their pain will be relieved or their need met. And just like the bat signal, your brand shines over and above your daily, weekly, monthly, and annual ad campaigns.

This is why branding is my second recommended step, not my last. You need to focus on your branding the minute you start thinking about your company's identity. In every meeting, with every investor, as you draw up your stationery and your business cards, you need to be thinking about branding.

Ask yourself:

+ How does this logo support our brand?
+ Does this business card support our brand?
+ How does our messaging reflect our brand?
+ What about the Web site?
+ Will this employee live our brand?

When people think about buying something, whether it's clothing or cola or cupcakes or closet organizers, you want them to use you as a reference for that brand. For example, at my house, we're a Southern family, a little bit country, but we call every soft drink "Coke." It doesn't matter if it's a Sprite, Pepsi, or Fanta. It's a Coke.

Why? Because that Coke brand is so strong that its name is synonymous with a refrigerated, chilled, carbonated beverage. Same thing with bandages. It's not "I need a bandage." It's "I need a Band-Aid." Same with gelatin. It's not "I feel like some gelatin." It's "I want some Jell-O!"

That's how you want consumers to think when you take over the world with your particular company. When they think about "socially responsible investing," our name comes up. It's on Google. It's on Yahoo! When people mention us by name in conversations, it's not by accident; it's because we've been pounding this brand for the last seven years and that's how we've defined ourselves: socially responsible investing.

In board meetings and brainstorming sessions, after trying out hundreds of keywords and mission statements and field tests and focus groups, we zeroed in on "socially responsible investing," not because we thought it would be the quickest way to fame and fortune, but because those three words defined everything my company wanted to do.

Once we had that definition, we could then move forward by branding ourselves using that phrase in everything we did. Every article, every interview, every banner ad and billboard and profile and classified ad and seminar and author bio we wrote included the phrase "socially responsible investing." That's why you need to know your identity early on and start branding immediately.

TAKE CARE OF YOUR BRAND AND IT
WILL TAKE CARE OF YOU

Your brand is your definition.

When people look you up, that's what they're going to see.

When you put your brand in the dictionary, it's going to be a description of what you are—as a company, as a person, as a team, as an entity, as a product, or a service. So you want to take great care of that brand because at the end of the day, your brand is also going to take care of you.

How? If you do it right from the very beginning, with careful thought and maintenance, your brand can and will be your company's greatest asset. Products may come and go—even Coke, Pepsi, Microsoft, and Apple have had miserable failures—but your brand remains. Your brand is going to be your calling card.

Your brand is going to determine whether or not you get the meeting with that big investor, or supplier, or wholesaler, or big box discount store. When people mention your brand in person, online, or over the phone, it's either going to make people smile or frown. Or maybe worse yet, have no reaction at all.

When people mention your brand in person, online, or over the phone, it's either going to make people smile or frown. Or maybe worse yet, have no reaction at all.

Remember, your brand is not just a logo. A brand is not just your mission statement or your tagline. When you roll out your brand, it is going to stick, good or bad. And nowadays when everything is "sticky," it will differentiate you and clearly state who you are.

The minute you launch that Web site, your bio goes live, the world sees your logo, and folks start logging on, your brand gets cemented in the public consciousness. So take great care and time writing down how you're going to be perceived, because those initial discussions lay the groundwork for your potential brand.

YOUR BRAND: One-Stop Sizzle Shopping

People are busy and, frankly, they don't care all that much about you. Hey, I want a nice, cold beverage when I reach for a soda. I don't want to know how much money went into the logo design, the advertising, the recipe, or the refrigeration requirements.

People want your product, not your drama or your process. That's the reality you're facing. They also don't want to be told they have to follow you all over the place to find out who you are or what you're about. I love social media, I love advertising, I love word of mouth, and I love PR. But what I love most is giving my customers the straight skinny, the down and dirty, in as few clicks as possible.

At its heart, that's what a brand provides. When your company logo matches your company text, when your message is repeated over and over, when they see the same smiling picture in the same ads again and again, eventually they won't even need to see all that stuff anymore to keep your brand alive.

That's because the Blockbuster Brand provides what I call "One-Stop Sizzle Shopping." Customers don't have to go a dozen different places to learn about you; your brand gives them all they need to know—all the sales "sizzle"—in one stop. In other words, your brand gives them everything they need to know about you whether they're looking at an ad or not.

When you've got a good brand, like Coke or Pepsi, the ads are merely reminders, visual stimulants to refresh that brand image in your mind. Over and above that weekly or monthly ad, your brand remains indelibly printed in the consumer's mind.

The reason you even had an opinion at all about Sprite or Bed, Bath & Beyond and the others in the Blockbuster Brand Test is because those seven or eight companies worked tirelessly to create a brand you would recognize and know the minute you heard their company's name. Yes, you can visit their Web sites to learn more, or get a coupon in the mail, or see an ad on TV, but all that is gravy because they've already worked so hard to establish their brand name in the consumer consciousness.

THE 5 MOST IMPORTANT QUESTIONS TO ASK ABOUT YOUR BRAND

A client I was working with recently was concerned about the success of the brand he'd built. (Emphasis on "built," as in he'd already built it before coming to see me.) The problem with his brand is that it's chained to the name and the image of his particular establishment, and frankly, it's not a very good one.

The colors don't match, there's no uniformity of thinking, no creativity or singular message being touted by his brand. So while he might have done a lot of internal brainstorming around this brand, he should have taken off the blinders and stepped outside the conference room once or twice.

Obviously he forgot to ask anybody else about this name and brand. My team and I were asking ourselves, "What in the world was he thinking?"

It can be frustrating when I run across a company like this so late in the game. They've spent so much money on their brand already and it flat out doesn't work.

Avoid this mistake.

Don't start asking questions about your brand when you're already so far downstream you can't turn around and go back even if you wanted to. Start upstream, at the very beginning of your journey, with the following 5 Most Important Questions to Ask about Your Brand:

1. **Is your brand easily recognizable?** I don't mean just the Nike "Swoosh" or the McDonald's "Golden Arches," but is the whole branding package—name, logo, letterhead, colors, symbol, etc.—easily recognizable? For example, you might not be able to tell at a glance what the Chick-Fil-A logo looks like, but you know the brand implicitly because of its famous chicken

sandwich, its waffle fries, its chicken-promoting cows. Likewise, I'm not sure what Papa John's logo looks like, but I get an instant "One-Stop Sizzle Shop" when I hear the name because I immediately associate it with the owner and founder's face and personality and its general "underdog" mentality. So this is what's so important about your brand—it's not just a logo, it's an identity. Make sure when people hear your company name, it stands for something and is easily recognizable.

2. **Can people understand it when they hear this particular brand?** Whatever you do, don't be so clever or arcane or cute or hip with your brand that nobody on the street knows what you're talking about. Be simple, be direct; less is more. Wendy's. Subway. Life is Good. Quicksilver. Apple. Amazon. Starbucks. These are brands that may not say exactly what they are in the title—would you know what Apple does if they didn't tell you?—but once you know them, you can instantly relate. Wendy's has that great little redheaded girl. Quicksilver is flashy and fun and youthful and surfing. Chick-Fil-A has those cows and is closed on Sunday. So you don't necessarily have to name your company "We Sell Subs" or "Buy Surfboards Here," but you do want a

name people can pronounce, say quickly and easily, and smile when they hear it.

3. **Can they easily input it and get to your Web site?** These days everybody has a Web site, but there are still times when someone hears your address or your brand name and doesn't have an opportunity to click to it until later. So make sure if you're on the radio talking about your company, or if people only hear your ad, they can quickly go to a browser screen, type in key words, and get your company. Some people come up with these crazy names and brands, but they sound similar to something else, or nobody can type them in correctly, and as a result, they lose thousands of online traffic hits.

4. **Is it something that people can easily repeat?** "Open happiness." That's the first thing you see on a Coca-Cola product—on the Web site, on a can, on a hat, in the movies, on a vending machine. "Open happiness." "Have it your way." It's on the wrappers, it's on the cups, it's on the Web sites and the commercials; it's Burger King. But take a look at these famous brands —they're not just slogans or logos. These phrases speak to the heart of the company's brands. Coca-Cola doesn't want you to drink just their cola; they want you to "open happiness." They want you to associate their drinks with fun, good times, backyard

barbecues, football games. Same with Burger King; they want the customer to be happy; they want you to "have it your way." So find a message the public can relate to and easily repeat.

5. **What is the essence of the company?** When you think about the Clif Bars, Microsofts, and Zip drives of the world, you don't have to visit their corporate Web sites or scratch your head thinking, "What is the essence of this company?" Clif Bars offer you protein and energy on the go for your active lifestyle. Microsoft offers you cutting-edge technology from a name you can trust. And Zip drives offer you portability to run your life from anywhere. Did these ideas, images, and emotions come out of nowhere? Heck no. For every positive vibration you feel from a company image, logo, ad or brand, that company spent literally hundreds of thousands of dollars and several years carefully crafting that message. When coming up with your brand, bounce your ideas off of other people. Find folks outside your industry, because you'll be surprised how many people think something may be hot because you're a computer guy, for example, but at the end of the day your target consumers will have no idea what you're talking about. So be very wary of creating a brand based on "just" your own world and ideas. Find

some focus groups. Find some friends. You can do it almost instantly on the Internet now by posting a free survey. Get on Facebook. Get on Twitter. See what thoughts and ideas are out there and get some brand feedback before *you* go out there.

DEVELOP A HABIT OF BUSINESS BRANDING FOR A LIFETIME

Companies don't just start themselves; people start companies. Strong, passionate, creative, talented men and women like you are the people behind the brands. So before you even consider branding your company, you must start branding yourself as an entrepreneur.

There's one entrepreneur in particular that I look up to. His name is Hubert Humphrey (no, not the late vice president). He sold his last company for about $700 million dollars. Every time he's touched something, every time he's involved, it's going to be a multimillion-dollar success.

How did Hubert Humphrey become a business brand unto himself? How about Gates, Madonna, Martha Stewart, Simmons, and Trump? How did these CEOs establish personal brands that have eclipsed their company brands?

THE 25-SECOND TEST!

WANT TO GIVE you a simple way to measure your brand to see if it's easy to articulate and memorable. Can you say what your company does within twenty-five seconds? If you're talking to someone and they ask what you do, can you explain it in twenty-five seconds in a way that is clear, concise, memorable, and impactful? In other words, does that person say, "Oh," and move on, or are they so compelled by what you said that they want to learn more? Find a local networking event and test it out.

Let me give you an example of a twenty-five-second pitch: "City Capital Corporation is a publicly traded, socially conscious financial firm that empowers communities through investments in green energy and housing in urban areas. Additionally, we help individuals make better decisions with their retirement through self-directed IRAs and other investment tools. Recently the *Wall Street Journal* ranked us as one of the top 100 most socially conscious companies in the world."

Wow. Now think about what you learned in such a short time period. You learned about everything we are involved in and that we made the *Wall Street Journal*. Based on your level of interest, you should be curious enough to ask follow-up questions.

They began with what I call a *personal* brand, a certain way of doing business and promoting themselves that eclipses the products and services they offer. And they used that personal brand with a business or product to become business magnates. Trump doesn't just build buildings; he builds an image that fills his buildings.

What contributes to his image? Books, lectures, seminars, TV shows, radio appearances, parodies, imitations on *Saturday Night Live*, hobnobbing with celebrities, the works. That's because branding isn't just a "job" or a duty or a chore to Trump; it's a habit.

It's something he does daily, habitually, naturally, to build his personal and professional brand. That's the goal I have for you, to get you in the habit of thinking not just in terms of product or service, but in terms of your brand as well.

As a company, you might produce many products or offer dozens of services at any one time. How are your customers going to remember them all? They're not. Do you know every single product, catalog number, product spec, or app name for everything Apple offers? Heck no. You just know that if it's Apple, it will be good.

So while you may have many products or services, you only have one brand. And that's the brand folks are going to remember. Your brand precedes you. If you do it right—and you will—that personal and professional brand will help you in all kinds of ways.

It will open doors, raise capital, secure advertising, get your name in the papers, and get folks to answer the phone, put on events, and buy your products—all with that "One-Stop Sizzle Shop" I spoke about earlier.

And one of the fastest ways to build a brand these days is through social media like Facebook and Twitter, the very definitions of branding in our popular culture.

It's all viral and all social media, all the time. They provide the platform and they work well. People use them, talk about them, and become what advertising experts are now calling "evangelists." That means you don't just use a product, you also tell everyone you know to use it.

The amazing thing about social media is that it truly starts online and then leads elsewhere. It transcends directly into the offline world, because everybody keeps talking about what they just said or posted or saw or heard online.

So how do you get a brand that everybody can keep talking about? It's something that goes back to the same thing over and over again—your brand must answer those five simple questions from the last section to be instantly seen, hard, recognized, understood, and translatable.

PUTTING THE 'ZIP' INTO ZIP DRIVE:
A Case Study

Back in 1994, a tech company called Iomega created one of the first portable storage drives ever to come out: the Zip drive. Now, nobody has seen a Zip drive in a long time, but if you remember, whatever latest-and-greatest high-end storage devices came out back then, everybody just called them Zip drives.

It didn't matter what brand it was, or what they called it, or how far they tried to distance themselves from Iomega, it was still just a Zip drive! Because Iomega was first and it branded its Zip device, everyone associated everything that came after with the Zip drive. They were all Zip drives.

I really like the Zip drive brand because it so quickly and effectively cornered the market. It became like Coke and Band-Aid and Jell-O—a product name that became a generic label. I find myself to this very day calling every storage device a Zip drive. I call those little USB discs and plug-ins Zip drives. Thanks to Iomega, Zip is branding at its best.

IGNORE YOUR BRAND—DOOM YOUR COMPANY

If you choose not to practice brand-building, you've just signed up to be in the audience rather than onstage. You didn't decide to be an entrepreneur because you wanted to be like everybody else. You're going against the grain as an entrepreneur, so why in the world would not you do the same thing with your own business? Why would you not brand that business creatively and give it its own identity?

If you ignore branding, you've essentially doomed your business to wearing the same blue suit with gold buttons and khaki slacks that everybody else wears. You're just blending in. You're fighting for slices of the same pie as larger companies with more resources, when you could be unique, with the potential to get an even bigger slice of the pie—or have a pie of your own. When Apple created the iPod, it essentially baked a new pie and had total control of the market. Apple could do that because of the brand it had developed as a company and the sophisticated strategy it used to brand the iPod.

What defines you as a business? What separates you from everybody else? If you can't define your unique selling brand, you've just hindered the growth of your company—and the sale-ability of it—significantly.

The difference between a $20 million company without a brand and a $20 million company with a brand is that one sells for $20 million and the other could sell for $1 billion. So yes, it is just that serious when it comes to a brand—which is why you ignore your own brand at your own peril.

MY BRAND, MY LEGACY

I have seen firsthand the power of branding in my own life and career. Now as I told you in the Introduction, I began my career as an Elite Entrepreneur at the ripe old age of twelve, designing video games and starting companies. I didn't know anything about branding then; I was just . . . Ephren.

And even though I wasn't even a teenager yet, I was wearing suits and building companies and doing these pretty outrageous things. However, none of it made a huge impact when it came to branding.

I was confusing a name with a brand name—until I hired my branding and PR folks, who told me we had to come up with what differentiated me, what commoditized me, what made me special.

So we looked at what I'd accomplished, and how unique it all was, and we settled on the "the youngest black CEO of a publicly traded company." Before, it was just Ephren. Now it was a brand.

When we came out with that, we raised some eyebrows and found our niche. Things just exploded from there. We got the book deals. We got the speaking deals. I've been in two movies. Other companies would kill for all the media and press that we get, but I didn't have to spend money on advertising because nearly everything got thrown to us for free.

Why? Because I was no longer just another kid with a name—I was a brand. We could approach news people, reporters, radio DJs, business editors and say, "Hey, we've got the youngest black CEO of a publicly traded company on the line, you want to take that call?"

They could see the potential immediately and answer, "Sure! I'll take that call . . ." It's the same way I got my TV deal; it's how we've been able to move so many books. We invested time in this brand.

Was it cheap? No. I spent hundreds of thousands of dollars in energy, time, and personnel developing and cultivating this brand, but I'm going to save *you* pretty much all that money by telling you how we did it, the mistakes we made, and how you can take it to the next level.

———————

PIMP YOUR BRAND!

One important step when it comes to branding is researching the legalities around the brand names you choose. We selected an amazing brand for me, the youngest-ever black CEO of a publicly traded company. I became known as a title I can't legally use here in these pages. Let's just call it "The *blank* engineer," where the blank stands for a very similar five-letter word that also begins in "b" and ends in "k" and is a common word for African-American. That title captured everything about me and where I wanted to go. It worked so well people would stop me in the airport and say, "Hey, I know you, you're the *blank* engineer." Well unfortunately, we received a letter from a company saying it had trademarked that term, and we had to immediately cease and desist from using it. Talk about a buzz kill. We had found something that worked, but we had to stop using it and go back to the drawing board.

The next thing I can't emphasize enough to you: Be ready if and when that brand "sticks." Case in point: When we first started our Urban Wealth tour across the country, it hit like gangbusters and we had opportunities flooding into our company because of this new brand that we'd established, but we didn't have the infrastructure to support it all.

And that's where the difference between a ordinary brand and a Blockbuster Brand comes full circle. Say you're out there with some new brand, plastering it everywhere, getting your name known, going hog wild. But if you haven't worked through the distribution channels, the customer service, the overriding philosophy of how you're going to engage the customers once they've recognized and rewarded your brand, then it's not a Blockbuster Brand, because all the pieces don't fit!

Remember, anyone can throw up some billboards and design a logo and get folks curious, but that's not monetizing the brand if there's no infrastructure there to catch the customers when they come calling. The reason you start thinking about your brand so far upstream is because you want all the pieces in place—human resources, customer service, research and development, production, shipping—in place and aligned so that every message you send is on message, on the same page.

If your brand is "the best customer service on earth" but folks get treated poorly when they call, you aren't monetizing your brand well, let alone producing longevity for the long haul, like a Coke or a Pepsi.

So, we developed systems and processes around this brand to not only keep it intact, but to also monetize everything it comes in contact with. We set up call centers. We wrote scripts. We trained the entire company to work the brand.

Remember, the brand can't just live and die with *you*. Even a personal brand morphs into a professional brand. Can you imagine Donald Trump hiring anyone who isn't going to further his brand, in any position, at any of his companies? Can you imagine Microsoft hiring mediocre employees to design their cutting-edge technology? The brand defines you; it lives and breathes in every corner of your company.

SIZZLING SALES:

*Discovering the Secrets to
Sales Success*

Every company has only three problems:

1. Sales
2. Sales
3. Sales

Seriously, if you can't sell it, then why are you doing it in the first place?

Unfortunately, the world is full of people with great ideas they can't sell.

The patent office is filled with registrations for products that will never hit the market. Why? Not because they're not good products, but because the inventor has no sales skills.

Without the ability to sell, you are dead in the water. No company exists without sales. All the bright ideas, branding, marketing, degrees, products, services, and parking spaces are pointless if you're not closing deals and making money.

In short, if you're not *selling*.

In this section, I'll teach Elite Entrepreneurs what I consider one of my most valuable skills, the ability to sell—to take any idea and sell it to anybody. If you look at every great entrepreneur story, it's always about how something was sold, sold, and sold some more.

Think of the personal brand names, the ones that speak for themselves: Diddy, Trump, Gates, Dell, Branson. These are Elite Entrepreneurs who aren't just selling products, they're selling themselves.

Some of them are all over the place. You've got Diddy selling records, cologne, clothes, cars—even vodka. You've got Richard Branson selling airlines, CDs, books, and cell phones. But the one thing both men are selling is a lifestyle, a certain philosophy that starts—and ends—with them.

Diddy sells the rock star, high life, glamor, glitz, style, fashion, class.

Branson sells the rebel, maverick, passion, excitement, risk, daring.

These words don't just describe a vodka or an airline or a record label or a fragrance. They describe the entrepreneur himself.

Even a Bill Gates, Donald Trump, or Michael Dell—people who specialize in one specific area of expertise, be it software, real estate, or computers—still do it with personality.

Bill Gates exemplifies cutting-edge technology and absolute social responsibility. You cannot think of Gates without thinking of his company's influence and, simultaneously, of his efforts to make the world a better place.

Donald Trump is about property, no doubt about it—hotels, golf courses, high-rises, commercial real estate, resorts, condominiums. But the man is so much more. He's a brand unto himself, a living legend who is also the consummate professional.

Michael Dell is synonymous with the entrepreneurial spirit; he revolutionized how people think about, design, buy, order, and even personalize their own computers.

As smart and talented, as serious and hardworking and revolutionary and entrepreneurial as these very diverse and individual men are, they all understand one basic concept of business: **the art of selling**.

Unless you want to stay in your garage selling your products and services to your mom—no matter how great those products and services may be—you have to learn to sell.

Even if you hire somebody to do it for you—and we'll talk about that in this chapter as well—being an entrepreneur is all about selling. Not just your great idea, product, or service, but selling yourself.

SELLING THE INVISIBLE STARTS
WITH SELLING YOURSELF

I often say that entrepreneurs are "in the business of selling the invisible."

That's because many of us start with just an idea, and we understand very quickly that not everyone else thinks in terms of ideas alone. Bankers, investors, engineers, accountants, CPAs, lawyers, foremen, even employees and customers, want black and white, numbers and logic, products and services—things they can see, touch, and feel.

But we entrepreneurs often don't have those tangible things yet; we're starting from scratch, with an idea. Imagine Diddy back in the early 1990s, explaining how he wanted to build a "multimedia conglomerate with multiple income streams across a variety of interconnected entities," while standing empty-handed in front of a bunch of bankers who had never heard of hip-hip and don't think much of rap. Imagine affable, handsome, charming, cheeky Richard Branson in a room full of stuffed suits, explaining how he wanted to start a luxury airline, a toy model in his hands.

Like Diddy and Branson, we have to "sell the invisible" in order to make people see how the reality will look, often months or even years before we'll have something to actually point at and say, "See, now *that's* what I was talking about!"

That's why selling yourself is so vitally important. When you walk into a room prepared to "sell the invisible," no one will buy it—*no one*—no matter how good the idea or product is, unless you can sell yourself.

Investors, partners, and bankers—the money people— already know what you don't: that business is hard, that there are roadblocks and obstacles you've yet to encounter, that markets are fickle, and customers are even more so. Don't get me wrong, they want to invest in risk because many times risk pays off, but they prefer a *calculated* risk. One thing that mitigates risk is the ability to sell.

If you can win over bankers and investors with a humble, homemade flowchart or a simple prototype, that means you can sell. And if you can sell an idea to *them*, chances are you can sell a product or service to the masses.

That's what they're looking for; that's what everybody's looking for.

That's what I'm going to help you give them.

WHEN IT COMES TO SALES, IMAGE IS EVERYTHING

To really sell yourself and your company, take your cue from Hollywood: **Image is everything.** You've gotta have the right look, the right style, and the right presentation before anyone will believe what you're selling.

For example:

+ Can you imagine Donald Trump living in a trailer?
+ What if Bill Gates gave his next press conference in a track suit?

Sales is all about presenting a consistent image, and Elite Entrepreneurs understand that when it comes to image, once you find what works, you stick with it. Image is reinforced time and time again through three things:

1. **Repetition:** Present the same image over and over and people start to associate that image with you. Have you ever seen Donald Trump looking anything less than immaculately dressed and perfectly coiffed? No, because he knows repetition drives image.

2. **Visibility:** To build an image, it has to be seen. So not only do you have to consistently build that image, but you have to let people see it. When you go to meetings, when you're in the paper, when you're around town, doing fundraisers, shaking hands, attending events, you should be the visible representation of that image. It's not enough just to

have a great image. If that image is going to help you sell, it has to be seen.

3. **Continuity:** The image has to be repeatable, comfortable, and continuous; that's how recognition builds. Decades after he got famous in the 1980s, Mr. T still looks like Mr. T. Same goes for Weird Al Yankovic and Hulk Hogan. Lady Gaga is the consummate image maker. Love her or hate her, the woman has a very distinguishable image that is cutting edge, fashion conscious, and absolutely trailblazing. That's because she reinforces her image through repetition, visibility, and continuity. Anyone can use this formula to create an image, starting today.

Trump's image represents his own personal and professional style; in many ways he dresses like his buildings—sophisticated yet flashy, sleek but stylish. His buildings are places you want to visit; the man himself is someone you want to do business with.

Bill Gates lets his work speak for him. A simple suit, a nice watch, clean shoes, and he's good to go. Why? Because he's not so much about style as he is substance. Still, he reinforces his image consistently in a very visual way.

So what is your personal and professional style, and how can you reinforce it over time so that it becomes a selling point for you, your idea, your product, your service, or your company?

It all starts with image.

I realize startups often don't have a lot of money, so we have to prioritize when it comes to image creation. But here are some ways to get it accomplished, even without a lot of resources:

Never underestimate the value of personal style

A friend of mine works from home doing network marketing and is extremely successful. He could wear anything he wants to work each morning—boxer shorts, pajama pants, gym shorts, his birthday suit—and no one would ever know. But every day he showers, shaves, and slides into slacks, a belt, a dress shirt, nice socks, and polished shoes.

He doesn't work in a cluttered basement or a modified garage with a dartboard on the wall or a spare bedroom with an exercise cycle in the corner. Instead, he works in a home office that looks like a regular office: big desk, bookshelves lining the walls, his diplomas hanging just so, state-of-the art office equipment, the works.

Why would he go to all that trouble when he's just running a simple startup from home? Because he has a very specific, professional, credible image he's going for, and wearing a suit and sitting in a CEO-style office immerses him in that image both physically *and* mentally.

My personal philosophy is if you dress like a slob, you're going to eventually act like a slob, and nobody wants to be in business with a slob! I joke, but I'm serious, too. **How you look—your clothes, your personal style, your grooming habits, even the deodorant and cologne you wear—matters.**

I'm not saying you have to be a Trump, a Gates, and definitely not a Gaga! If you work in a business where wearing overalls or shrimp boots makes the right impression for your investors, co-workers, and clientele, by all means, wear them. Knowing yourself—and your audience—is the first step to selling an authentic, personalized image. This is why at City Capital our employees wear suits at all times, even on plane rides. After all, you never know whom you're going to meet and when.

It's not about trying to be someone else; it's about trying to be the best you can be. That's what "elite" means: being the best of the best.

Hand them something that counts

Know what a business card is?

It's an opportunity.

Yes, it's a small piece of card stock with some contact information and a name, but it's so much more. I'm always disappointed when someone hands me a plain old business card with no pizzazz. I'm half as likely to call that person as I am the one who hands me a business card that has style, with funky colors or a new font or a clever catchphrase or a different size or shape.

Same goes for a press kit, a brochure, a business plan, or any other piece of information or media you hand to someone. The next time you design a business card or brochure, think as if you're walking into a fine boutique and picking out a suit or a dress for a night on the town.

But this is no regular night on the town; you're picking out some duds for a ritzy dinner party on New Year's Eve with fancy, famous people in attendance. You wouldn't pick out just any old pair of khakis and powder blue shirt for a night like this, would you? Well, that's what you're doing when you're handing someone a generic, do-nothing, say-nothing business card, pamphlet, or brochure.

I have printed millions of business cards, flyers, brochures, leaflets, pamphlets, press kits, and calendars in my day, and I've found it costs just as much to be boring and bland as it does to be memorable and creative.

If you're going to spend the time and energy to write and print a hundred-word description of your company, why rush it, why sleepwalk through it, when with just a little more effort you can create something magical, creative, and memorable? Remember, your brand never sleeps; everything goes back to image, from the convenience of your visitor parking spaces to the sound of your receptionist's voice to the printed materials you hand out.

Can you imagine someone like Diddy or Trump handing you a generic black and white business card with no style, pizzazz, flair, or personality? I bet theirs are sleek, shiny, maybe with foil and a memorable slogan or quote on the back.

Don't think of your printed media as a chore; think of it as an opportunity.

Every opportunity counts, so always **hand them something that counts.**

The image should translate well

When it comes to image, I say "put like with like." In other words, things should match, always, every time. Look at Target; I love its image, it's so sleek, it's so consistent, it's so . . . red!

Can you imagine seeing a purple Target ad? Or yellow or pink or blue? From the shopping carts to the signage to the clearance stickers to the employee shirts, Target owns red and lives it. The ads are vibrant, new, fun, energetic, passionate, and creative, just like the color selected (no doubt very carefully) to symbolize the company's corporate and consumer philosophy.

You have to think the same way: make it match, keep it consistent, put like with like. For example, if you live in the mountains and your company promotes eco-friendly walking tours through some of the last indigenous forests on the planet, you're not going to show up on location in a three-piece suit and a briefcase and hand out foil business cards made with some potentially hazardous chemicals.

You're going to show up dressed appropriately: hiking boots, cargo shorts, and olive green T-shirt. Your business information will be printed on your fishing cap because that's more "environmentally friendly" than handing out non-recyclable business cards. That's what's appropriate for you in that setting because of what you're trying to do and how you're trying to do it.

- **Company dress code:** If you're selling eco-friendly clothing free of harmful dyes and synthetics, why have your salespeople show up on cold calls wearing synthetic suits and drinking out of Styrofoam cups? Remember—like with like. For an image to resonate, it first has to translate into every facet of your company.

- **Printed material:** If your style is flashy, big, and loud, then naturally all of your printed material should match that style, reinforcing your image even when you're not around to reinforce it personally. Your business card is a way for someone to take you with them, wherever they go. Shouldn't it look, feel, and sound like you?

- **Corporate style:** Even if you have no money, you can still look and act like a billion-dollar, Fortune 500 company *if* you act and spend very carefully. Make sure your Web site is clean and well-edited, that the links work, that your business cards and brochures are impeccable, and that your sales staff is well-groomed, etc. These things don't cost a lot, but they represent your image well.

- **Reception and assistance:** Even if you're starting your company from your garage, there is no excuse for not having some type of receptionist or virtual assistance. Even if you outsource this stuff, or just use your mom, dad, sister, brother, spouse, or fiancée, you can and should have reception and assistance that matches your personal and professional image.

Words have meaning

No matter your budget, no matter what you have to barter, trade, or promise to make it happen (within reason, of course), find a way to make sure every word you put out there for yourself is camera-ready and not just some "sloppy copy" you dashed off overnight.

A potential company's or employee's material should never include bad grammar, typos, or misspelled words. If you can't sell yourself when it comes to putting out your own message, if you can't do something simple like proofreading your Web site, business card, or brochure, how are you going to sell yourself when a big deal is on the line?

Hang out in the right places

Sell yourself where it matters. You can't please everybody, nor should you try. Nike is not marketing itself to couch potatoes, the same way Krispy Kreme isn't marketing itself to triathletes.

Know your strengths and define your target audience; then go where they are. If you're marketing to kids, go where the kids are. If you're selling to seniors, hang out where they hang out. Craft your image accordingly.

For example, when you're selling to kids and you hang out where kids hang out—the Internet, malls, movie theaters, concerts, skate parks, etc.—you want an image that reflects their values, interests, and style. The more you inundate yourself with this stuff, the easier it will be to come up with a style that "fits."

WANT SOME PRESS?
START WITH A (PRESS) KIT

I know press kits aren't exactly the sexiest thing to talk about when discussing entrepreneurism, but when it comes to sales, you can never get enough exposure. You get exposure through favorable press, and to get press, you need to start with a press kit.

Everyone has ideas about what should go in a press kit, but here are some of the elements I always include in mine:

- **Talking points:** Get together a short list, maybe six or seven statements that tell what your company is all about. These are short, brief, single sentences that speak to the heart of your company, your people, your product, and your social commitment.

- **Company info:** Include your company brochure here, with pictures of corporate personnel, relevant contact information, FAQs—anything you think might help a reporter, freelancer, or webmaster write about you in his or her paper, Web site, ezine, blog, etc. Remember, press kits aren't for bragging, but for making it easier for others to give you press. (Otherwise they'd be called bragging kits.)

- **Community involvement:** Talk about what you're doing in the community, the schools you partner with, your professional and personal affiliations, the groups you sponsor, and the fundraisers you've thrown. If possible, include pictures and, preferably, video (see below).

- **Testimonials:** You'll want to show you have happy clients. For example, people who have used your product, who have tested your product. And if you don't have any such people, give your product away and then get a few testimonials from the people you've given it to.

- **Stickiness:** These days you can't always physically "hand" your press kit to people, and in some cases, they prefer to view it online anyway. I think this is a great opportunity for you to get "sticky" and include some interactive, audio, or video components in your press kit. For example, YouTube and Viddler (and other sites that will exist by the time this book is printed) make it easy for you to upload video content for potential investors, reporters, webmasters, reviewers, clients, and customers. You can upload videos of focus groups, of happy customers using your products, of reports of you working in the community or partnering with a school, etc.

POLITICIANS AREN'T THE ONLY ONES WHO CAMPAIGN!

People who run successful companies appreciate the value of a good sales campaign for creating Sizzling Sales around a specific product, service, launch, redesign, time of year, etc.

Campaigns are not generic; they are specific, timely, personalized, active, and above all, passionate crusades or specific promotions that build around a single event. For example, you can build one sales campaign to launch your company, but that campaign won't fly six months down the line when you're at a new phase of development.

You can build sales campaigns around any number of things:

- **A new product launch**
- **A new package design**
- **A new logo or slogan**
- **A new CEO or corporate restructuring**
- **A new initiative or growth spurt**

One of my first sales campaigns was for a company I started which I called My First Dot Com Company. It was one of the first job search engines for young people.

We started with a $250 marketing budget to develop a brand around this young, funky company that was helping students find jobs.

So we thought about it and finally came up with an entire campaign to promote our company like a party. We drafted up these flyers—funky, fresh, colorful flyers. We took them to high school parking lots, and when our primary consumers came out of class at the end of the day, they'd find our flyer on their cars.

Lots of the kids threw them away, but not the kids who needed spending money, whose parents had been on their case about finding a job, or who were saving up for college. We also developed a PR campaign around the brand that was socially responsible. It focused on two teens helping other teenagers find employment; it was a "feel good" story.

Every parent was interested in that, but also every teenager. We had hit both our consumers and also second-party advocates (parents) by having a third-party endorsement from the media. We ended up building a $3.4 million firm off of this brand by using savvy, guerilla marketing in a basic grassroots campaign.

Although the campaign seemed loose and casual with a funky, fresh, party atmosphere, it was actually very calculated and slick. As a result, we became synonymous with helping teens find jobs. We may have defined the youth market category, but we also attracted a fleet of copycats who came behind us and tried to play off of our brand.

So an effective campaign has some specific requirements:

- **Define the campaign:** You don't just start a campaign; you work on it for a while first. We spent a lot of time planning the preliminary campaign for our My First Dot Com Company concept, bringing in branding and PR experts to help us not only identify the target audience but also figure out how to reach them. Yes, putting flyers on cars seems simple, but so many factors went into it—what to say, what color to use, the latest slang, which schools to hit, at what time, etc. So before you start the campaign, you define the campaign by asking:

- *Who is it for?*

- *What do they need?*

- *How do we reach them?*

- *What will appeal to them?*

- **Launch the campaign:** I love the word "launch"; it's like blasting a rocket into space, and that's just the kind of energy and enthusiasm you need for any campaign. You launch a campaign by treating your campaign workers like customers: wine them, dine them, finesse them, get them as jazzed about this campaign as you are about your company. It's a lot to ask: post flyers, get shopkeepers to hang up posters, hand things out to people. Money isn't the only incentive folks need. So launch this campaign properly by building it around enthusiasm and energy.

- **Own the campaign:** A campaign is short-lived and temporary, so when you hit it, hit it hard and then get out. Passing out flyers is great, simple, easy, and effective, but only temporary. After a while it stops being fun, funky, and fresh and starts being a nuisance and a chore. You either have to end the campaign or switch gears and adapt. Either way, you must own that campaign: You must be the only company doing it—flyers, sandwich boards, fundraisers, whatever—so you dominate your target audience with this one, singular message.

- **Leapfrog the campaign:** Campaigns are like playing pool; you don't just shoot the ball willy-nilly to sink it. You line up one shot so that after you (hopefully) sink that shot, you're set up to sink the next ball as well. So "leapfrogging" is what you do when you're phasing out one campaign while ramping up another one. You'll always have to be doing some kind of campaign to create Sizzling Sales.

SELLING AND RE-SELLING:
Creating the Boomerang Brand

Creating a strong brand contributes to selling on many different levels. I like to say that your brand is "selling that never sleeps." The very word "Trump" now stands for a distinct and distinguished personal brand that is singular and personal to one man.

Another crucial aspect of branding is something I call the "Boomerang Brand." As we all know, boomerangs are hunting tools that come back after you throw them. Throwing a spear or shooting an arrow is a one-off; it either hits its target or it doesn't. And it doesn't come back. Boomerangs give you multiple opportunities to establish your brand because **they always come back to you**!

Likewise, every little marketing piece you do is branding, supporting that brand, and at the end of the day, driving sales back in to monetize that brand. So anything that you do with your brand has to be true to that brand; it has to get the message out and make sure it represents and elevates that brand. But at the same time, anything you do put out must be bringing something back.

That makes it a boomerang brand. You throw it out, and it brings something back. I throw my brand out, it brings something back: recognition, press, testimonials, symbolism, attention, sizzle, steak, whatever. Your brand never sleeps because you're always sending it out there, and it's always bringing something back to you.

It may not pay off today or tomorrow, but when your brand is strong, it will pay off. Who do people vote for? The names they recognize the most. Whose names do they recognize the most? Those with the strongest brands.

How do consumers "vote"? With their wallets.

HITTING THE BULL'S-EYE WITH YOUR TARGET MARKET

You can waste a lot of precious time and energy if you're creating an image and a brand but are selling to the wrong target audience. And if your target audience is too broad, you'll have more competition.

Elite Entrepreneurs must always strive to find that hidden market, or that hidden slice of an established market. For example, one of my new clients is a multimillion-dollar software development company that has carved out a very specific niche for supply chain management software, specifically for food distribution companies.

Many companies need supply chain management software, and a lot of generic, template-driven products exist to tap this market. But this client's software is solely for food distribution companies. Now that's a huge market, but not one that has tens of thousands of players competing for the same slice of the pie.

Becoming an Elite Entrepreneur is about finding those hidden opportunities and going against the grain to capitalize on them.

Look at it this way: When you're a lion stalking its prey in the wild, you can't go after every wildebeest grazing on the plain. You've got to be selective, pick one or two that look the weakest, the slowest, the oldest, the youngest, then chase them down. That way you increase your odds of success.

Too many entrepreneurs come to me and say, "Everybody will want this product!" Maybe, but a better path to success is instead to tell me, "Every single food distribution company in the Midwest will need this personalized product." Now you're not chasing a thousand wildebeests; you've chosen your perfect target and have honed in on it.

How do you hit a bull's-eye on a dartboard? Not by going for the black rings on the edges or the green and white rings farther in, but by zeroing in on dead center and letting it fly. Hey, you may not hit it every time, but when you're aiming at the right spot, your chances increase considerably.

When we were looking at our retirement business for self-directed IRAs with City Capital, we first thought, "Hey, it's going to be all the people who are retired." But, that wasn't our target market. Why? Because they are so set in their ways.

There is a psychological aspect to understanding your target audience. You can't just be a bean counter; you have to be a psychiatrist and a sociologist, too. What is it about this audience that will make them want your product? How can you, and you alone, give them something nobody else can?

Those are the questions we asked with our retirement audience. We realized they were resistant to innovation, even though they had the qualified funds, so we determined this wasn't the best audience for us to zero in on. In addition, it was the most difficult and most expensive audience to go after, because everybody was targeting it.

So we slowed down, backtracked, strategized, brainstormed, and started identifying people who were a little bit younger, in the thirty-five to fifty-five range. Those are the folks who had the assets to invest but needed those assets to grow it if they were to hit their "magic number" for retirement. They were also young enough and innovative enough to understand our product. They realized they had to do something different from what everybody else was doing to get where they needed to be. And that's when our story—our personalized, targeted, niche story—really resonated with them; they loved the "social mission" aspect of it.

Even though the retiree crowd had more money to

invest, it was a lot easier—and cheaper—for us to go after that younger market. We've now carved a niche with a very select, very specific audience that matches our product with their needs. This is the supreme value of knowing your target audience—putting like with like.

How does this translate to sales? Well, you find a target audience and then tailor your sales message specifically to that target audience. Our sales force will be specifically designed, informed, trained—and even hired—to go after those targeted customers with a product perfect for them.

It's going to be cheaper, easier, and much more profitable to go after a specific niche than trying to conquer the whole world. Again, it's the one wildebeest versus a thousand theory. So, Elite Entrepreneurs, you need to focus in on that one wildebeest you want to eat tonight versus the whole herd. That way you'll always be full.

Sales: The Entire Company's Responsibility

Who is responsible for sales?

That's an easy one: **The entire company is responsible for sales.**

At City Capital Corporation, it doesn't matter if you're the receptionist, in client support, or an intern on your first day, you'd better be able to sell. We are an ABC company—Always Be Closing. It is our operational core.

We're selling every time our receptionist picks up the phone. In fact, we don't even call them receptionists anymore. We call them Directors of First Impressions, because for the client, that's what they are—the first impression.

Remember, it all goes back to brand and image. You need to have the image established companywide so you can actually provide the service somebody's calling about.

Technically, your sales force is responsible for the closing of day-to-day sales, but that's just a formality. At City Capital, my job—my actual title—is to be the company's CRO, or Chief Rainmaking Officer.

That means it's my job to make sure that our brand is there, that our market is there, that I support my staff, and that I'm out there selling, too. Every book I write, every radio show I'm on, every business card I hand out, every hand I shake, every dinner I eat, or every waiter I tip or cab ride I take, I'm ABC: Always Be Closing.

■

You can always find plenty of operations people, but you can't always find good sales people. Hire them early and train them well.

■

Our entire company is built for sales. As I said earlier, in a company there are only three problems: sales, sales, and sales. You can always find plenty of operations people, but you can't always find good sales people. Hire them early and train them well. And make sure all your employees know that everyone at your company can and will sell.

Or they'll be working for someone else.

WHEN ENTREPRENEURS CAN'T SELL, THEY HIRE!

Okay, okay, I realize not every entrepreneur is a born salesperson.

Look at Bill Gates; he's certainly not a strong-arming, slick-talking, ABC salesperson. But he's got the smarts, the know-how, and the instincts to hire people who are strong salespeople, people who'll take his ideas and run with them.

Does he still qualify as an Elite Entrepreneur?

Well, what do you think?

Unlike Gates, my superpower is sales. I have been selling since before I could drive because it comes so naturally. But I also have some weaknesses as well. Operations, for example. Some entrepreneurs are great at operations and terrible at sales. So what do you do when you do a lot of things great, but sales isn't one of them? You find that person who does enjoy sales and you bring him or her on board.

No matter how great your image is, no matter how well-thought-out your brand may be, no matter how grand, innovative, and ambitious your sales campaigns are, if you can't negotiate, if you can't deal with people, if you can't close the deal, you've just wasted a lot of people's time—yours, your employees', and your customers'.

Every company needs a rainmaker. If you don't have a rainmaker on the team, if that wasn't in the business plan, then that has to be the number one draft pick. That's the guy or gal who throws touchdowns, that's the guy or gal who puts the money in the bank. If you aren't bringing the money in, you've just got a dream and a vision, and your company will be on death row within a couple of months.

So bring in rainmakers quickly, cheaply, and efficiently. And if you have to, give them a piece of the action they'll be bringing in. Rainmakers are priceless, and you'll see your results in real time long before they'll see theirs.

THE SECRET TO FINDING NATURAL SALESPEOPLE

A natural salesperson is going to be extremely per-sistent. As soon as you file your corporation papers, they'll be calling on you, selling themselves and selling you their company's product or service. So notice the people who are calling on you and observe how they sell themselves.

Every time the Aflac agents come by my office, I'm trying to get them to work for me. Why? For four simple reasons:

1. They're bold enough to walk into our office on a cold call.
2. They've got the right look, the right presentation.
3. They understand selling to executives—it's a corporate service that requires many calls to get a sale.
4. They're sales people. They're looking for an opportunity, one that can help them build money but also residual income. They're terrific potential recruits.

If you're staffing your sales force, start with your own front door. Recruit the salespeople who are calling on you. Why? Because they not only have experience, they have the courage to cold call you. And, if they actually sold you something, they could be somebody you want to hire. Believe me, every salesperson who calls on City Capital gets recruited.

BRINGING THE TEAM TOGETHER:
Dominating the Field with the
Right Sales Force

Regardless of whom you hire, be it a born salesperson or just a devout believer in your product or service, you need a sales force that is so hungry, so ready, so passionate that they will go out into the marketplace and dominate the competition.

I talked earlier about launching a campaign; you need to "launch" your sales force the same way. When I talk about sales, I get fired up because I know how desperately important it is to have a burning, driving, dominating sales force. Everything—all of it—rests on sales.

If you're not selling, you're dying. If you're not closing, you're losing.

That is why having a brand, an image, a uniform message, and product that's a winner is so important. The right salespeople can pick and choose for whom they work. Why? Because they can sell anything. Just as I go after that Aflac insurance agent every time he visits me, other folks are going after him, too.

Good salespeople aren't just selling a product, they're selling themselves. You want to believe in yourself so strongly, to present your company so uniformly, to announce your product or service so confidently that sale-people will be jumping up and down to work for you!

What you're going to need is a sales force that has that fire in the belly. If you've just hired some nine-to-five salesman who won't do cold calls, won't go out in the rain, won't get up early, won't stay late, who just wants to sit in the cubicle and work the phones, well, you've probably got the wrong person.

The great thing about startups, the great thing about being an entrepreneur, is the cause. The cause is the idea, the mission, the social justice, the drive to succeed, the profit.

Everyone should not only *get* the cause, they should be firm believers *in* that cause. You want receptionists burning to come into work every day. Look at Pam from the TV sitcom *The Office*. She didn't want to simply answer phones—she wanted to sell. Eventually she got her shot, but only because she proved herself by selling every day of her life, regardless of her current position.

I said earlier that everybody is responsible for sales at your company, and that's because everyone should believe firmly in the cause. Especially with your formal sales force, you need reps who truly believe in the company and aren't just there to pick up a paycheck.

You need some team players—good *volleyball* team players. I love volleyball; now *that's* a team game. To win at volleyball, you have to work as a team. Good volleyball players know how to set up a shot and play off each other's strengths and weaknesses. They know how to pass, dig, serve, and kill—all as a finely tuned unit, as a team.

WRAPPING UP WITH PRE-SALES:
A Word from T. Harv Eker

Where do all sales start? Upstream, with careful planning and lots and lots of pre-sales. One of the books that influenced me early on in my career was T. Harv Eker's classic *Millionaire Mind*. Eker says, "If you can't pre-sell it, you can't sell it when it's ready." This is priceless advice.

As I said earlier, if you can't sell it first, then why are you doing it? Pre-sales are a great way to test the business model to determine if you've got a hit. When I was starting Goshen, my biofuel company, we went out and sold a few million gallons before we even built the plant. The same group that was buying that fuel in advance came to us and said, "Hey, one of our other partners has a plant. Will you please take it over and use it?"

So not only did we pre-sell fifty million gallons to them, they were now going to give us the plant to make their fuel! As Mr. Eker said, "If you can't sell it now, you won't be able to sell it later." We definitely sold—pre-sold—that fuel.

HEROIC HIRING:

*Everything You Need to Know to Handle
Human Resources like a Pro*

e've established that no matter how elite you are as an entrepreneur, you're not going to be able to do it all by yourself. Every leader needs people to lead, and there are only so many hours in a day. Unless someone has discovered a way to clone people by the time this book is published, you are going to need help.

At a startup, of course, leaders take a hands-on role in more areas than at a more developed company. So while you may be stuffing envelopes and shaking hands and answering phones and assembling do-it-yourself desk chairs, you can't spend all your time doing daily tasks if you're to lead a startup company to success.

So what do you do? You assemble a great team, and that means hiring the right people. In my opinion, hiring is one of the biggest challenges for entrepreneurs, because not many of us are born leaders.

Yes, we have a vision and sure, we have passion and

definitely we have commitment, but we too often assume everyone shares that vision, passion, and commitment when in reality, most folks are just looking for a paycheck. Kimberly S. Reed, CEO of Reed Development Group (www.thereeddevelopmentgroup.com), says, "As a leader you have to do three crucial things when sharing your vision with your stakeholders and team: *define* the vision (this is the seed of self-leadership); *live* the vision; and *communicate* the vision authentically and realistically."

The challenge for entrepreneurs becomes believing in yourself enough to make tough hiring decisions, even if it's not your forte. You must put the right people in the right jobs at the right time, and not just hire everyone you meet because they're nice or need a job.

Your company is not a charity, and while I'm all for giving back when there is a surplus, most entrepreneurs are strapped for cash to begin with, so now is not the time to make charitable hiring decisions. Hiring the wrong people will quickly turn you from a business to an NFPB (not-for-profit business). Instead, be very clear about whom you want to hire, what jobs need to be filled, and the type of person you are looking for. This chapter will help you attain success through heroic hiring.

THE 3 MOST VALUABLE ASSETS OF AN ENTREPRENEURIAL EMPLOYEE

To start you on your journey, I've identified what I call the 3 Most Valuable Assets of an Entrepreneurial Employee:

- **ASSET 1:** *Passion*

Look for employees who have the same sense of passion you do. They may not have the same experience in business you do, but as I like to say, "Passion is career blind." In other words, you can drop passionate people into just about any company and they won't just survive; they will thrive.

Experience can be overrated. For example, you may be leading a company that's producing a product no one has ever seen before, so if you hire on experience alone, your talent pool is going to be mighty shallow. Instead, hire on passion, and trust passionate people to learn as they go.

- **ASSET 2:** *Drive*

To succeed in any business, in any position, at any pay grade, employees need drive. I can walk into any office at any of my companies at any time and see who's driven and who's not. Driven people are always on task; you can see it in their demeanor, in their discussions, in their dress, and even on their résumé.

You want to hire people with drive because, in the beginning, you can't always hire experienced, senior-level folks because you simply don't have the funds or proven track record to give them what they require.

Instead, you want to find driven people who are at a point in their lives where they want to work hard for something they believe in, even if they can't see their results right away.

I'm not saying hire only young people, though young people are often driven. I'm saying hire people who are *young at heart*. Maybe they've been kicked around by the economy and need to start over—and startups are great places to start over.

Maybe it's a housewife whose kids have left the nest and who's eager to start a new phase in her life. The point is, driven people will willingly share your passion and commitment, regardless of their age or experience-level.

■ ASSET 3: *Commitment*

Finally, regardless of age, education, or experience, make sure to hire people who can get behind your company with the same level of commitment you have. This can be a challenge because, after all, this is your baby, something you've cooked up and dreamed about all on your own.

So seek out like-minded people. If your company is involved in saving the environment, seek out folks who are committed to going green and sell them on your ideas and solutions. Even if your company is a straight-up capitalistic business selling sneakers or shirts or soap, find the thing that makes it different—what made you start it in the first place—and sell them on that.

Remember, when your "company" is little more than a spare room, a garage, or a mostly empty office suite, you're not going to be selling prospective employees on perks or trappings they can see. What you're really selling is yourself. So you must be someone your employees are willing to commit to. How? By showing them how committed you are.

Now that you know what type of person to hire, let's discuss the various hiring challenges you face on your journey to becoming an Elite Entrepreneur.

■ PAY TO PLAY: *Hiring on a Budget*

It's a challenge for any company, but particularly for a startup company. Most startups have limited funds, and even those with angel investors or larger budgets should be wary of relying on nothing but money when attracting new people.

As discussed above, you need people with passion, drive, and commitment, regardless of age, experience, or education. Remember, this is a startup, so you may not want the most experienced employee from an established company—someone who feels more qualified to run things than you are.

I'm not saying experience isn't valuable; it absolutely is. But hiring the *right* person—not the most experienced person—is more likely to pay off for you. So throw out all those HR programs you studied in your MBA classes and pay attention to what it really takes to hire the right folks at the right time for the right startup.

***

So throw out all those HR programs you studied in your MBA classes and pay attention to what it really takes to hire the right folks at the right time for the right startup.

Here are some of my favorite tips for hiring on a budget:

- **Hire hungry:** Find people who are hungry. At City Capital, we like people who have youth, energy, and something to prove. Individuals who are extremely well-established may not be a great fit for a startup environment. You're going to need people who are young, hungry, and looking to take themselves and a company to the next level. They're eager to demonstrate their talent and their worth. They're hungry.

- **Hire 'em on the rebound:** We have had success hiring people who have lost jobs at other companies and after months on the market looking for similar work, came ready to get back to work and eager for that fresh burst of creativity only a startup can provide.

- **Hire grateful:** Look for people who want to work. I frequently sit in on job interviews at my companies and am frustrated by the occasional applicants who act like we're doing them a favor by hiring them. I'm always grateful for the opportunities life has given me, and I want to work with people who feel grateful for the opportunities I've given them. Grateful people don't take things for granted, and they're some of the best workers I know.

- **Hire happy:** I like to work, and I like to work with people who like to work. We all work hard here, but we like the work and that makes us one thing: happy. Am I saying there is never conflict, strife, anxiety, or stress? Hardly, but when you like what you do—and the people you do it with—life, work, and profits are that much easier. When you hire, hire people who seem happy, positive, and upbeat.

PERMANENT VS. PART-TIME:
The New World of Outsourcing, Freelancing, and Contract Help

As we begin this section, it's important to remember that at a startup, nobody will ever be permanent—not even you or me—once the company is no longer a "startup" but a proven entity. So keep that in mind as you begin your journey through the hiring process.

We have been trained that employees are on-site, that they earn a salary, get insurance, sit at a desk, enjoy lunch breaks, and head home at five o'clock. We were brought up in a world where our parents worked in offices full-time, but the world is changing and new trends like outsourcing, freelancing, and work-for-hire contractors are revolutionizing the way people are hired—and the way companies are run.

When we start a new company, we try to outsource everything. Go freelance, go contractor. That way you don't build up massive amounts of overhead that will drain the resources you need. Here are a few examples of how valuable temporary, off-site, or freelance help can be.

Let's say you've booked a big trade show in the fall, and it's going to be a great opportunity for you to show off your company, products, services, whatever. Naturally, you want a brochure that puts you in your best light. Just as naturally, you have no one on staff to write, illustrate, bind, and ship such a thing.

You can outsource this job to a couple of freelancers. Start with the writing, since that is likely to take the most time. Reach out to local folks in your network, if you know of any, or hit up a site like www.elance.com or www.guru.com to post the project.

Find someone who has written similar brochures and who can do the job in the time you need. Ideally, try to get someone who can also locate some royalty-free photography and lay the brochure out as well.

With your writing and illustrations covered, you now need a printer, one who'll most likely bind and ship the brochures as well.

Why would you hire a full-time staff writer and possibly illustrator, let alone set up your own printing plant, when you can outsource this very doable job to able, willing, and affordable freelancers who will be happy for the work and who, if they do a good job, can become your "go to" folks for future writing, graphic, and printing needs?

Meanwhile, remember that when you do outsource, you are doing so on a simple work-for-hire, contractual basis. No workman's comp, no insurance, no liability, no overhead—you just hand off the work, make a small deposit, get the work back, and, when/if you're satisfied, pay the balance.

Let's look at another outsourcing scenario. You have a slightly bigger project this time, one that needs a little more hands-on help, but still doesn't require a full-time commitment. Let's say you want to use social media to promote your new company, but you have neither the expertise in this area nor the time to fully commit to such a project.

You do some searching and realize you can hire a social media specialist to help you use Twitter, Facebook, You-Tube, and others to your advantage, but it's not something that can be done overnight. In fact, it's going to require a three-month commitment to get to the point where the consultant can "hand it back" to you to run it on autopilot.

In this scenario, you don't need someone on-site, but you'll want to monitor your consultant/contractor frequently, because as opposed to the brochure job, which probably took three weeks, this is a three-month position and of vital importance to the marketing and promotion of your company.

In both cases, however, you're outsourcing a fundamental service to proven professionals without the added overhead, liability, and insurance required for a full-time professional. What you have, in essence, is a full-time employee who will be filling a short-term need.

This is why hiring is so crucial—and potentially problematic—for the startup entrepreneur. Rather than hiring a dozen full-time people you don't need, you may end up hiring twenty or thirty independent contractors in the course of a year—CPA, bookkeeper, lawyer, writer, illustrator, printer, Web developer, etc.

The good news is that hiring freelancers and other outsourced help will give you plenty of practice when it comes time to expand and hire the actual full-time help you need to meet your goals.

PERMANENT STAFF:
Pros, Cons, and Considerations

In this day and age, particularly when it comes to startup companies, I consider permanent staff a luxury not a necessity. Certainly there are many good reasons to have full-time, committed people working for you, but don't bring them on until you're more established, until you're further along on your path to success.

Think about it: When you've got permanent staff, they're there all the time. There are payroll, disability, insurance, and liability issues you've got to consider every two weeks. It's nonstop. It's going to keep coming and coming and coming and coming.

So make sure that your business is stable enough to support that ongoing commitment, and make sure you've got adequate financing to cover not only your full-time staff but also the other surprises and obligations that are sure to pop up every day in the life of a new startup.

On the other hand, when you have temporary, free-lance, and contract staff, they're there for a specific purpose, for a predetermined time frame, at an agreed-upon price. And even those parameters can be adjusted, up or down, if conditions change.

But with full-time payroll commitments, there will be major blowback if you are forced to adjust and revamp: disgruntled employees, back pay commitments, maybe even legal troubles.

So in the beginning at least, outsource, outsource, outsource as much as possible. If you can outsource performance-based transactions or monthly billable hours, it'll be that much easier to manage cash flow and allow you to extend financing terms, giving you the flexibility and breathing room you're likely to need.

And here's a bonus: If your contractors, vendors, and freelancers are well-respected, well-known, and talented, they're probably working for other companies around town, doing similar tasks. If so, they are a networking gold mine. Many are the deals we've gotten thanks to referrals from our contractors, who put us in contact with the movers and shakers we needed.

LAYING DOWN THE LAW:
Letting Freelancers, Vendors, and Contractors Know Who's in Charge

Recently our company sent out a memo to all of our vendors and contractors to let them know that their relationship with us was performance-based and that when there was no performance, we'd prefer they not bill us.

Here's a copy of the memo:

July 1, 2009

Dear Vendor:

This letter is to inform you of upcoming changes in City Capital Corporation (CCC) Contracts and Accounting Department practices. CCC is a publicly traded company and required to maintain specific policies and procedures mandated by the Securities and Exchange Commission (SEC) to properly inform all stockholders of operations and accounting functions within the company.

As a result of recent internal audits by the executive management team, following are process enhancements that may affect your relationship with City Capital Corporation effective August 1, 2009:

Active & Fully Executed Contracts and Agreements—All vendors, consultants, and partners are required to have a fully executed agreement on file with City Capital Corporation. Further, the period or performance or contract period must be current to be considered as "Active."

If your current arrangement does not meet the aforementioned guidelines, please do the following:

Submit your company's proposed contract or agreement with a detailed description of your service offerings and a breakout of cost. If your company will bill CCC hourly, please include the hourly rate you are proposing in your agreement. All proposals will be evaluated to determine suitability for CCC business needs, and requests for revisions or modifications will be directed to your designated contact. Once approved and signed by your company, CCC will fully execute the agreement with two company signatures, one being that of an executive officer and the other a designated contracts specialist.

Note: CCC will not consider any agreement that does not contain a standard 30-day termination clause. Also, CCC will not enter relationships requiring a standard monthly retainer be paid.

Invoicing & Payment—All vendors, consultants, and partners are required to submit for approval monthly invoices prior to City Capital Corporation's remittance of payment. Only approved invoices will be paid and all invoices will be paid on a Net 30-day payment schedule from the date of approval. Your invoice must be detailed (see invoicing guidelines). If additional information is needed prior to approving your invoice, the accounting department will contact you immediately for resolution.

City Capital values its relationships and is committed to paying vendors, consultants and partners in a timely manner; however, to avoid delays in receiving payment please adhere to the following invoicing guidelines:

Invoice Guidelines
- Have a fully executed and "active" agreement on file
- Cost and services must match the scope of work contained in your agreement

- Describe services provided or tasks completed
- Itemize services rendered by date
- Breakout of cost by service
- Provide hourly rate and number of hours to coincide with services rendered (for hourly rate contracts)
- Attached or submit receipts for reimbursement of purchases
- Unit cost of products (if applicable)

Note: CCC will not pay for services rendered in the normal course of your business operations.

Invoices may be submitted electronically via fax or mail.

Submit To:
Electronically: porth@citycapcorp.com

By Mail: Attention: CCC Accounting, 2000 Mallory Lane, Suite 130-301, Franklin, TN 37086.

By Fax: 888-216-8858

Regular Performance Reviews—to ensure continuous service improvement, feedback, and open communication regarding performance and expectations, CCC will require quarterly evaluations for all vendors, consultants and partners.

You will be assigned an operations point of contact (POC) who will be responsible for working with you on the outcomes of services you provide for CCC. Quarterly, the operations POC will schedule a time to meet with you to discuss key performance indicators, make recommendations, and discuss effective ways to enhance services. A documented vendor evaluation form will be completed and filed with the contract. This form will also be sent to the vendors for their files.

By implementing these new procedures, we anticipate a more efficient and productive relationship with our partners. Should you have any questions or concerns please feel free to contact our office at 877-367-1463 or email info@citycapcorp.com.

Sincerely,
Wendy Connor, Chief Operating Officer
City Capital Corporation

It was a friendly if blunt way of saying, "Hey guys, City Capital here. We've enjoyed working with you in the past but are not quite sure why we keep seeing monthly recurring bills for work that wasn't even done this month. As a reminder, please invoice only for billable hours as a work-for-hire contractor."

The message was two-pronged. First, I wanted to remind these day players that they weren't full-time employees collecting a monthly paycheck no matter what they did or didn't do that month. Also, because we are a public company, we must be compliant and answer to our shareholders. And that's exactly what the memo affirmed we were doing.

The memo was a good thing for us because it made us start outlining very specific terms of payment: how we were going to compensate and work with our clients and our vendors, and exactly how we needed information submitted. By formalizing procedures and putting a structure around everything, we could make sure that we'd be able to maintain adequate cash flow and cease being drained by contractor bills and invoices. Remember, even outsourced help can become a cash drain if you don't stay on top of it and know who exactly is doing what, for how much, and how often.

Make sure that you define how you work with vendors; don't let the vendors define how they'll work with you. You're paying for the service, so you are el dictator, in no uncertain terms. Make sure that you exercise your power and your rights in an authoritative manner. Because at the end of the day, they need your business, not the other way around.

If that particular freelancer can't do your brochure on your terms, there are dozens more just as capable and affordable who can. If that social media consultant is bleeding you dry, make sure you have an "out clause" in place so you can bolt before you give away the farm for something that's just not working out.

Have a standard agreement you use with contractors, one that covers you but is simple enough for them to understand without consulting a lawyer of their own. Use your contract, not theirs. Make it fair, but always make it fair to you first.

DON'T LET THE DOOR HIT YOU ON THE WAY OUT: When It's Time to Turn Hiring into Firing

I am fairly firm with the people I work with. I perform daily and expect those I work with to perform daily as well. When they aren't, don't, can't, or won't, it's usually not going to fix itself, and rarely do I have time to fix it.

I make strong hiring decisions based on instinct—or trust others to do the same—and prefer to do the hard work of hiring downstream rather than upstream. So when someone isn't working out, I know nothing short of a miracle is going to make things right. And that's when I nip things in the bud.

Again, this is why it can be so challenging for entrepreneurs. Startups are intense. Working ten or twelve hours a day, six or seven days a week, believing in something, starting something together—all that creates a family atmosphere where folks are reluctant to fire "family members" even when those people aren't performing as they should, or must, for the survival of the company.

But hiring and firing people comes with the territory; it's the landscape of a successful entrepreneur. This is one more reason to outsource as often as possible; the ties don't bind quite as tightly!

For example, when vendors stop performing and they really aren't delivering what they said they were going to deliver, cut them off immediately. Do not wait. Do not mull it over. Drop the axe and get somebody else. That becomes even more critical in the startup phase. Make sure you select the right people the first time, because you don't have the time, energy, or resources to do it over and over again.

As we discussed earlier, get every single one of your contractors under contract. And make sure those contracts include a non-disclosure clause and a non-compete clause. You don't want them snatching your ideas or your customers.

Put in place the right processes, procedures, and forms so everybody understands clearly what they're supposed to be doing, when it's supposed to be done, and how they'll be compensated. Accountability is the goal for both sides. You want no misunderstandings.

If you don't have those things in writing, signed and understood by all parties involved, you'll have a contractor relationship that will drive you instead of you driving the relationship.

FREELANCING: It's a Vision Thing

As an entrepreneur, you probably realize by now how few people actually believe in your dream. Sure, your friends and family are on board with your "vision," but most people want to hear more about results *now*, not the results later. Particularly when it comes to hiring, most folks aren't really willing to work for a wing and a prayer and a promise.

Every company goes through its trials and tribulations. Good times, bad times, in-between times. Fast times, slow times. City Capital is definitely not immune to all of that, nor are any of my other companies. But at the end of the day, when you have vendors, sales people, staff, employees, contractors, etc., who believe in your vision, who believe in the brand, they will rise to the occasion when tough times come.

An employee who's just there for the paycheck will most certainly cut and run if you ask them to stay late, work harder, do more, give more, and be more. Those who share your vision, however, even if they're only vendors or contractors, will feel your pain and make it theirs. They're in it for the long haul, even if payment—and satisfaction—is deferred.

That's why it's so critical that you define a culture with your vendors and contractors that tells them you're not just a paycheck. You're building a company and they're building it with you.

PARTING WORDS ABOUT HEROIC HIRING: The Decisions You Make Now Affect the Bottom Line Later

Final words on "heroic hiring": Never rush or be pressured into making a hiring decision. As an entrepreneur, it's easy to get cornered, because the margins are always so thin, the deadlines always so tight, and the pressure always so great. But never forget, you always have another twenty-four hours to step back, count to ten, take a breath, and make the best decision.

It can be tempting to hire this or that vendor, freelancer, or even full-time employee because he or she looks good on paper or says all the right things or because you need a warm body to fill that order by Friday night. But even hiring the wrong freelancer for the right job can set you back if you don't pump the brakes and make the right hiring decision beforehand, not after the fact.

We all make hiring mistakes, and I've certainly made

mine. My biggest mistakes—my most costly mistakes—were made in haste. I've done just about all the wrong hiring moves I wrote about in this chapter. So learn from my mistakes before making your own.

The tools in this chapter should help guide you in your own hiring decisions, so don't throw them out the window or ignore them when you're in a hurry or you have to make several hiring decisions all at once. Practice only makes perfect if you actually practice, so keep this chapter handy, and when it comes to heroic hiring, stand your ground and be a hero!

6

GENERATING GROWTH:

The 3-Step Plan to
Innovation, Joint Ventures, and
Strategic Partnerships

arly in my career, one of my mentors told me something that forever changed the way I look at the life cycle of a business. I had always assumed it took several decades—or at least one decade—for a company to fully mature, but this wise, successful businessman told me that if your company hasn't taken off in *seven years*, don't spend another day trying to make it happen; shut the doors and bar the windows immediately.

At the time I thought he was crazy! Today, in my own experience, I often tell people, "If your company hasn't exploded in *three years*, shut it down immediately. Go put your money and time into something with more potential, because this obviously isn't working."

Why do I make such outrageous claims? Because I'm not talking to your traditional, everyday entrepreneurs; I'm writing for Elite Entrepreneurs. And if there's one staggering difference between traditional entrepreneurs and Elite Entrepreneurs, it's that Elites' companies experience a growth explosion within three years or less.

Blowing up in three years or less takes a lot of work, but it's not impossible. In fact, most of the people we work with do have this kind of success, because once they embrace this three-year growth schedule, they find that generating growth is very achievable.

The key to this supercharged success is "accelerated growth." You don't just grow like a normal six-foot sunflower; you grow three times as tall—in half the time!

This has been the key to success in all my years of business strategizing: grow, grow, grow. Have you ever seen one of those little shark, turtle, or superhero toys you submerge in water at night and when you wake up in the morning it's grown to ten times its original size? That's what I'm talking about with your company's growth.

There is one driving secret between how I suggest you accelerate your growth and what most business "gurus" recommend: The easiest, fastest, and cheapest way to double, triple, and pretty much blow up your profit margin and grow exponentially—sometimes overnight—is through strategic partnerships and joint ventures.

We'll be discussing both in this chapter. Let's start with joint ventures.

THE ABCS OF JOINT VENTURES

A joint venture is one organization coming together with another organization in a mutually exclusive partnership to accomplish a common goal, vision, or mission. (Hopefully resulting in great profits for both companies.)

Let's say your company provides seed packets to retail garden store chains all over the country. You're very good at what you do and demand is high, but profits are flatlining and you'd like to do something to increase revenue. A marketing brainstorming session comes up with the perfect solution: Add branded gardening tools to your product line to supplement the corner of the market you already dominate.

Great! There's just one problem—you don't have the expertise, facilities, materials, or any idea how to produce gardening tools! No problem, you find a company that *does*, and you forge a joint venture with it to produce your tools for you. This is good for both companies. Not only do you get your problem solved without adding a new factory, conveyor belt, metal shaping machine, packing and shipping, etc., but the tool manufacturer can simply do more of what it already does in a broader market by aligning itself with you.

The beauty of, and secret to, successful joint ventures is making them win-win scenarios for both parties. If it's not a mutually beneficial partnership, then it's not a partnership at all; it's just you hiring some company to do a job.

For example, we created a joint venture with Verde Bio Fuels for the production and development of fuel. Verde agreed to buy all of our supply and stock for us, which gave us a great customer and a client, but it also gave us leverage to get our own facility built. What's more, Verde would sell and market the product as well. This company was a terrific joint venture partner because it had expertise working with and selling to municipal clients, expertise it would have taken us decades to acquire.

What did Verde Bio Fuels get out of it? Simply put, we had expertise in bringing together other municipalities and forging government relationships, thereby getting access to markets it couldn't. And because it was a true joint venture partnership—a win-win—we agreed to split the proceeds.

Remember that to partner with someone, particularly in a joint venture, is to create a mutually agreeable relationship where both parties profit. (Otherwise you're really looking at an employer-contractor relationship, as we talked about in our last chapter.)

Joint ventures allow you to inject new energy into your organization because of a certain skill set or expertise you have forged over the years. For example, we're currently developing an iPhone application that stemmed from somebody coming to us with a great concept but without the expertise to get it built, developed, and tested. We had all that—and capital as well.

That said, don't be afraid to aggressively state your own needs and affirm from the get-go what you want out of the relationship. Find companies that are a good fit for you, where the two of you merge like puzzle pieces. Everyone has strengths and weaknesses; **the goal is to find a company whose strengths overcome your weaknesses and whose weaknesses need your strengths.** You'll profit quickly, reaching what I call accelerated growth in record time.

6 SECRETS FOR A SUCCESSFUL JOINT VENTURE

Joint venturing isn't always easy, and it's not without its complications even when things do go smoothly. But with the 6 Secrets for a Successful Joint Venture below, your path should surely be easier than mine was.

SECRET 1:

Know What You Want out of the Partnership

Have you ever wandered into a busy doughnut shop with no idea what you want, other than . . . a doughnut? There are so many rows of doughnuts, and they all look good. After a few minutes trying to make up your mind, you notice those in line behind you are getting restless, and the cashier is impatient. So you make a rash decision and order something that may be good, but not exactly what you had in mind when you walked in.

Talk about buyer's remorse.

While finding a joint venture partner is obviously a tad more important than choosing a doughnut, you can see the same kind of dilemma here: If you don't know what you want in the first place, how can you possibly expect to choose the right partner?

Before you find a joint venture partner, determine what you really want out of the partnership. Clearly define your role—what you bring to the table—as well as that of your potential partner.

You also want to consider for what you need a partner. Again, if you just need a simple part produced, or a brochure written, or royalty-free graphics for your Web site, you don't need a partner—you need a freelancer.

So think long and hard before entering into a partnership and only do so when you have clearly defined roles that outline the expectations, requirements, and "job descriptions" of and for any potential partner.

SECRET 2:

Know with Whom You Want to Partner

Next, figure out the kind of partner you want to deal with. Not just "someone who produces garden tools" or "someone with expertise in producing biofuel," but the type of *person* you want to partner with.

In the next few sections, we'll talk at length about potential partners and five specific traits to look for. But for now, take out a sheet of paper and write down the type of partner you want to work with.

It may seem silly, but it's a good exercise. For example, if the words you use to describe an ideal partner are "strong," "firm," "not wishy-washy," "decisive," and "blunt," you are obviously looking for a very specific type of person and should concentrate in these areas.

SECRET 3:

Find the Right Partner

Finding the right partner is important to a successful joint venture, so you should spend much of your time here in the search. After all, with the *right* partner, the rest of these secrets naturally tend to work themselves out.

How will you know when you've found the right venture partner? That's like asking how you'll know when you've found the right business to be in, the right invention to invent, or the right passion to pursue. You just know.

Yes, absolutely, it's possible to make mistakes, but the harder, longer, and more seriously you look for the right joint venture partner, the more likely you are to find the right one after all. (See the 5 Great Places to Find a Potential Venture Partner later in this chapter.)

SECRET 4:

Get to Know One Another

Time is always of the essence, but as you begin to work with your joint venture partner, build in some time to get to know one another. Take a trip, or a retreat, or hunker down over a weekend of takeout food and work out the kinks in your professional relationship.

Introduce each other to your families, go to lunch or dinner, or simply play a round of tennis or golf. Partnerships are like any other relationship; when they grow in a vacuum (like simply working together) they often crumble when exposed to the everyday struggles of life. Instead, **get off on the right foot by creating a relationship first, and a partnership second.**

SECRET 5:

Get to Know Your Market

Now that you have created a successful partnership, work together to understand your market. In our earlier example of a garden seed company joint venturing with a gardening tool manufacturer, the partners had to determine how to share the target audience in order to double, triple, or even *blow up* sales.

For example, maybe your gardening tool partner sells its tools in a market, store, city, or state you've been wanting to break into for years but with no luck. Well, here is your in! Likewise, see how your seed connections can help their tool-marketing efforts.

Win-win.

SECRET NUMBER 6:
Get to Work!

Once you've created a partnership and the two of you have agreed upon a road map of where you want to go, you must take that first step: begin the journey together. Pick a start date for your partnership and stick to it. Set clear goals, job titles, and expectations and stick to them. Have metrics and checkpoints in place to keep you both on track.

For example, if spring planting season is your debut launch for your first series of branded gardening tools, work backward to create a realistic schedule—with built-in flexibility for emergencies—so that you can both work proactively toward your goals. Then check in regularly to make sure you are both meeting your goals. If not, regroup and see what can be done to get back on track.

5 GREAT PLACES TO FIND
A POTENTIAL VENTURE PARTNER

While it may seem daunting to find someone as important as a venture partner, you won't have to look far to discover like-minded success stories right around the corner, be it online or on your street.

Here are five great places to start:

1. **Social Networking:** Join social networks that are about nothing but partnering, whose members know the lingo of partnerships and joint ventures. LinkedIn is a good place to start, but branch out as you delve more into this challenging but lucrative solution to accelerating your company's growth.

2. **Your Business Organization(s):** What professional organizations do you belong to? Naturally, you've got your local Chamber of Commerce, your regional this and state that, so use them. Oftentimes we join such organizations and never fully use all the many resources at hand. Visit their Web sites, subscribe to the newsletters, or simply attend functions. You'll quickly find a variety of resources devoted solely to helping you find a joint venture partner.

3. **Your Database:** Why search outside when you can start inside? How many people are in your database? Five hundred? Five thousand? Fifty thousand? Instead of Googling "joint venture partners," first go to your database and see if any profiles match your needs. Imagine one of your own contacts hearing from you about a possible partnership!

4. **Your Customers:** Customers are a great resource for joint venture partners, particularly business-to-business clients.

5. **Mentor Groups:** I have made no secret of my love for all things mentor-related. Finding a joint venture partner is the kind of request mentors will eagerly help you with.

PARTNERING FOR FUN AND PROFIT:
The Beauty of Strategic Partners

Joint venturing is a pretty hard-core business relationship in which two companies come together to merge into an official entity. On the other hand, strategic partners are just that—partners who merge for a particular project, without necessarily forming a business together.

Strategic partners are individuals who can come to the table pretty much ready-made and bring something you need but, thanks to them, for which you won't have to hire full-time employees. For example, we may have a branding strategic partner or a marketing strategic partner—somebody who shares our strategic vision, our strategic plan, and our goals for growth—but is non-competitive. When we come together, we combine forces to make it happen.

Now, that might sound a lot like when you needed that brochure done and hired a freelancer to write it, another freelancer to illustrate it, and one more to print and bind it. But those are jobs; strategic partners fill an organizational gap you have.

Anyone can hire a PR person to manage his or her publicity needs, but **with a strategic partner you're not hiring out, you're partnering up**. So when I bring in a strategic marketing partner, I'm not paying that person some big retainer or monthly check; I'm partnering my services with his. I need his marketing expertise, and perhaps he needs my financial expertise, or he needs a business strategist to grow his company to the next level. He helps me, I help him—we're partners.

And in this way we can both experience accelerated growth, because I don't have to devote my time to marketing and he doesn't have to devote his time to business strategy. We both accomplish our goals in half the time. This is how companies are able to not just grow but to "blow up" in three years or less, through accelerated growth via strategic partners.

I love comic book superheroes. When it comes to strategic partners, think about a Batman and Superman team. Batman has no superpowers, but he has all the fancy gadgets, the intellect, the resources, and the know-how to truly be an asset as Superman's partner. Meanwhile, Superman can fly and has brute strength, but lacks the funky gadgets and overall mastermind brainpower of a Batman.

And that right there is key to the magic of strategic partnerships. Yes, you can do fine on your own and grow over time. But do you have the time? Do you have the energy to do all the things your strategic partner could do, practically overnight, because that partner is already an expert in the field?

Superman could certainly do fine on his own without Batman, and Batman could do just fine without the Man of Steel. But why not partner up with an expert in an area you're lacking and truly *accelerate* your growth, not simply grow?

DOUBLE YOUR PROFITS WITH HALF THE EXPENSES WITH POWERFUL PARTNERS

One of the secrets of accelerated growth: When you find those strategic partners and joint ventures, they're actually bringing their resources and their money to the table to help bring your product to market.

Take a closer look at QVC or the Home Shopping Network. They are veritable breeding grounds for joint ventures. First, you have an inventor with a product. Sometimes that inventor is the greatest salesperson in the world and the station will let them on the air. But if the station realizes the person isn't the best pitchman, it will loan that inventor someone who is. I call this the Pitchman Partnership.

QVC or HSN will use their platforms and marketing efforts, and millions of dollars in TV time, to put your product on the air. They take a percentage of the resulting sales because they've given you the venue and the professional salesperson. The inventor, of course, gets the exposure, the legitimacy, the sales—an immediate infusion of capital. In addition, the inventor often ends up with a massive retail distribution deal. Talk about accelerated growth!

The same thing occurs with major infomercial powerhouse Guthy-Renker. It will find a product and use its TV, branding, and expertise to launch that particular product, and will take massive royalties as well. What's better for the entrepreneur? To sit at home with a basement full of innovative flashlights or grills that nobody ever sees or uses?

Or to swallow that pride, let somebody take it over, put George Foreman on the case, and make $300 million? The choice is yours, of course, but the Elite Entrepreneur realizes that at the end of the day, it's about making sure the vision is accomplished, the brand is established, and the dollars are made. And he can move on to the next venture. Elite Entrepreneurs are successful at building, crafting, and selling companies, not nurturing lifestyle businesses.

THE 5 WINNING TRAITS OF
A PARTNERSHIP PERSONALITY

What is a Partnership Personality? In my experience, not every partnership is built to last. Many factors go into a successful partnership, not the least of which is personality. So before entering into a partnership with someone, consider the following 5 Winning Traits of a Partnership Personality:

TRAIT 1:
Flexibility

Ideally, you want to partner with someone who is flexible and who has been in business before—maybe even in lots of businesses. Try to find another Elite Entrepreneur, because an Elite Entrepreneur is more likely to work nights and not worry about working only nine to five or giving up vacation when you need him or her the most.

Entrepreneurs are flexible almost by definition; partners should be, too. As you interview and interact with potential partners, test them for flexibility. If they freak out at the prospect of changing a simple lunch date, conference call, or meeting time, how will they react if funding falls through or the production line shuts down?

TRAIT 2:

Patience

It takes time to get to know your partner, let alone partner successfully, so if that partner is "champing at the bit," make sure it's for all the right reasons. Yes, we all want to make money—and lots of it—but we all know that the secret to making money is to plan, plan, and then plan some more.

Build time—and plenty of it—into your schedule for choosing and meeting with a potential partner. Take it slow and create a professional atmosphere from the start. Chances are you two will click and be of the same mind when it comes to planning and pacing, but you'll know very quickly if you aren't. Better to know now, not later.

TRAIT 3:

Creativity

Look for those who are creative, not just in how they run the business, but in how they communicate and present themselves and their company. A successful partnership is always a creative venture between two like-minded individuals.

I like to work with someone who is an "idea person," a very creative, talented, and accomplished individual who never looks at something straight on, but instead looks at it upside down, backward, and underneath.

TRAIT 4:
Innovation

It's important to partner with someone with new ideas, new energy, new enthusiasm, and, most of all, new twists on how to get things done. Partnering accelerates your growth because it takes two great minds and puts them together. And that should make things go twice as fast, not slow things down.

■

Partnering accelerates your growth because it takes two great minds and puts them together. And that should make things go twice as fast, not slow things down.

■

What's the use of partnering with someone who simply does things the same way you do them? What you're looking for is a devil's advocate, a friendly nay-sayer who will question why you're doing what you're doing and offer new ways to speed things up.

TRAIT 5:

Fun!

Partnering isn't easy, and partnering with someone who isn't fun makes an already challenging proposition down-right dour. It's not wrong to have fun with your partner; in fact, I consider it a must.

PARTING WORDS ABOUT
ACCELERATED GROWTH: Keep Your
Vision in Focus, or Put the Brakes on Growth

Companies are kept from accelerated growth when they lose their vision and focus. They chase too many things that bring no real synergy or benefit to the market. What stops so many entrepreneurs is not having the right resources or access and not having the right partners.

We all know there are a lot of great ideas and companies out there, but oftentimes they have no sales department, they have terrible customer service, and they really haven't created those accelerated growth platforms and partnerships we've been talking about.

Many people try to build it out organically and slowly, but why build something organically if you can just latch onto somebody else's infrastructure and become a parasite entrepreneur and a parasite millionaire? Use somebody else's infrastructure, time, and money. Those are the rules to building wealth: other people's time; other people's money. The same thing goes for business. Use other companies' money, other companies' brands, and other companies' resources to help build your brand and make millions of dollars. That's how you get it done—by crafting partnerships.

What's more, when you craft the right partnerships, all of a sudden you have built instant credibility for your brand. A mentor I was reading about created a $100 million oil company using none of his own money. How? He created a shell corporation, partnered with a big oil company, and together they landed a government contract.

Now, he made "only" $90,000 off of the deal, but suddenly he had a $100 million company backed by a major international oil conglomerate. The oil conglomerate got another client that it normally didn't have. They crafted the joint venture and got the government contract because he had the resources, but he leveraged that and later took his company public for $400 million, all off of a $10,000 contract.

The lesson here is this: Focus on your vision at all times; never lose sight of what you want to achieve; and always build partnerships around the reason you got into that business in the first place.

CORNERING CASH:

Cash Flow Explosion Strategies

ash flow is critical to the success of every company.

It's not hard to understand cash flow; if you have no cash, then you've got no flow. In other words, nothing's happening. Everything in business takes cash, from hiring people to buying chairs to printing brochures to creating mockups to marketing to social media to the light bill.

Many entrepreneurs stick their heads in the sand about cash; they partner with a money person or hire an accountant and assume there's always going to be money in the bank, regardless of what the bank statement says. I'm not saying you should preoccupy yourself with money 24/7, but cash really *is* king, and without cash flow you're going to end up a pauper!

Some entrepreneurs are good at raising money; others are good at spending it. The truth is, we all have to spend it someplace, so if you're not good at making money, you need to be good at saving money. That all relates to cash flow. If not a lot is coming in, you can make the best of what you have by traveling budget class, using media mail instead of first class, refilling your own print cartridges, etc.

Every dollar in counts, just like every dollar out counts, and you can't hide your head in the sand about this stuff if you expect to be an Elite Entrepreneur.

That said, this chapter is all about Gargantuan (Financial) Growth, or how to capitalize on cash flow.

IT'S NOT ALWAYS ABOUT THE MONEY, IT'S ABOUT RELATIONSHIPS

Now, before we get to the money, let me talk first about knowing your needs. Yes, every entrepreneur needs financing, but you have to determine *how much* financing.

After all, if you're dealing in intellectual capital—books, music, media, TV, radio, whatever—and you're running around leasing office space and buying grand furniture and imported bamboo wallpaper, do you really need that much financing? Couldn't most of your work be done from home?

One of the best ways to manage your cash flow is to know your needs. Understand what you have to have, what you'd like to have, and what you can do without. If you're manufacturing garden tools or barstools, you'll need supplies, raw materials, machines, and people to put the tools or stools together. If you're in the ideas or music business, you may need only a basement office and a really great laptop and considerable hard drive space.

This may not seem like critical information, until it's time to pay the rent on all that office space you absolutely do not need. That is why cash flow is so critical but is also so solvable.

I work with entrepreneurs all the time, and here is something that might reassure you: 90 percent of startup companies don't need money. They need the right relationships. In other words, if your passion is greeting cards, and you want to go up against the likes of Hallmark and American Greetings, well, there are basically two ways to go: Finance yourself to the hilt and be in debt until you make a profit, or develop relationships to help offset your cash flow.

What do I mean by that? Anyone can run out to the bank and get financing and use that money to fund a company. That's basically like racking up your credit cards to the hilt and hoping that, one day, you can pay it all back —at 21 percent interest!

And I'm not saying that won't work; it's worked for a lot of entrepreneurs, and worked well. But it's stressful enough starting a new company without the added anxiety of all that debt load.

Besides that, let's say that you were to get a ton of

financing, have a huge influx of cash to start this greeting card company, and . . . then what? You rent office space; buy printers; hire artists, writers, graphic designers; do a deal with the local post office for reduced shipping; and . . . what next?

You still have to get people to buy your cards, stock them at the grocery store, in the drugstore . . . at Walmart! So now you have this warehouse on hold, all those printers gathering dust, writers and artists creating greeting cards without a market. All of it waiting for you to form those relationships.

Or you can start slowly with whatever cash you have on hand. Maybe you work out of your home office for a while; maybe a friend is a great artist and will work for next to nothing; maybe you find a writer from eLance. com. This way you're not out a ton of cash while you continue to work on your contacts at Walmart or Target.

Maybe your cards don't get into the big-name stores just yet; maybe you start locally and sell a few dozen cards a week in brick and mortar stores. Or maybe you create a free Web site with your first six greeting cards and market the heck out of it through social media, building a loyal, if small, following.

So you create six new cards, market those, and soon you have more followers. Suddenly stores start getting in touch with you, and you're getting some cash flow coming in. Now you can invest in those printers, hire some new writers and artists, etc.

In other words, don't put the cart before the horse by borrowing huge sums of money without yet having anything to sell or produce. Consider our first scenario: If you don't even have one single greeting card to sell, why in the world are you trying to get hundreds of thousands of dollars in financing?

Start with relationships instead—some local contacts, some creative talent, a mentor, a business lawyer, an accountant, your friends, family, and neighbors—and branch out from there.

Money isn't always the answer, because having a ton of cash doesn't necessarily teach you how to run a business. Instead, pretend you have *no cash* and find alternatives that way. Later, when cold, hard decisions require cold, hard cash, you can get what you need.

19 WAYS TO BOOST YOUR CASH FLOW TODAY!

Don't think getting a loan is the *only* way to inject a little cash flow into your company. In fact, there are hundreds of ways to get financing for your startup, and here are nineteen ways to inject some cash into your company *today*.

1. **Keep your day job.** If the orders aren't there and the product isn't available yet, keep working until the last possible minute so your regular paycheck can help support your startup.

2. **Pre-sell your product, idea, or service.** If you can pre-sell the product to the right group, and you have already researched and found the right manufacturer, you can take those invoices and turn them into most banks and get financing against those invoices. It's called factoring.

3. **Sell some assets.** Do you really need that second car right now? Or how about that antique grandfather clock or hand-carved headboard? eBay.com is great for infusing your company with hard cash by selling off assets you don't actually need. And hey, when things go better, you can always buy them back!

4. **Take on venture capital.** Do your research and be comfortable with the idea of giving up equity in your business.

5. **Get a bank loan.** It's always worth sitting down with a loan officer and pleading your case.

6. **Partner up.** If cash really isn't flowing and you're having a hard time funding the startup even using

the other eighteen ideas listed here, you may want to look for a partner who can take on some of the cost, as well as some of the work.

7. **Get freelance work.** If your entrepreneurism has to do with intellectual property, such as writing or coaching or producing, offer your services out on a consultant basis to keep money coming into the startup.

8. **Downsize.** If you look hard enough, there are hundreds of ways to downsize your life, from making your coffee at home to skipping movies for a month to taking the bus.

9. **Work a side job.** If you've quit your day job thinking you'd need all your time to work the startup, don't be too proud to work a side job while you get your new company off the ground. Find something you can do at night, if possible, like security work or waiting tables, so you keep the daylight hours available for your business.

10. **Sell off some investments.** If you have a second home, time-share, or stocks or bonds, sell some off in a timely manner at the best price possible.

11. **Find an angel investor.** If you can find such a patron investor, use that money wisely.

12. **Cash out that IRA.** Sure, there may be a penalty, but better to use your own funding first if at all possible.

13. **Borrow from your 401(k) plan.** Check how much is in your 401(k) and how much is available to take out. Cash out if possible.

14. **Put it on a credit card.** It's been done before—people have cut albums, opened warehouses, ordered material, even financed entire movies on their credit cards.

15. **Tap into your insurance.** Some policies let you "cash out early" or borrow against what you've paid in, so talk to your insurance agent about your options.

16. **Hit up strangers.** Put up a Web site to plead your cause and spread the word, asking for donations from strangers. It's desperate, but if you check out the legalities ahead of time and are straight-up about your needs, a few donated dollars here or there might just tide you over!

17. **Check out a person-to-person lending site.** A place like LendingClub.com might just be your answer.

18. **Get a cash advance.** See how much cash is available on your credit cards.

19. **Hit up the pawn shop.** How many spare TVs, CD players, iPods, radios, and watches do you need? If you're in dire straits and in fear of closing up shop on your new startup, better to get pennies on the dollar at the pawn shop than see your dream go down in flames. You never know when that last $500 is going to buy you the time you need to find success.

Regardless of whether any or all of these ideas work for you, the difference between traditional entrepreneurs who let their dreams fade because of lack of funds and Elite Entrepreneurs who struggle through the hard times to eventually find success is *creativity*. Sometimes you have to get creative with your finances to cover the next shipment, payroll, or insurance premium.

Before you give up, sell too soon, go bankrupt, fold, or shut your doors, check the above list one more time to see if there is an alternative way to make a quick $100, $250, or $1,000 to tide you over. In startups, a day, a week, or even a month can be the difference between no sales and turning the corner to success.

If you try hard and fail, there's no shame; but if you try hard and fail simply because you didn't look in every nook, cranny, and corner for an extra few hundred dollars to keep you in business for one more month, well, there's nothing very "elite" about that.

GOING PUBLIC: Exit Strategy or Financial Starting Line?

Running a company includes several phases. The one we've been most concerned with so far is starting up, where all hands are (constantly) on deck and cash flow is king. Now I'd like to address what happens when exiting a company, i.e., going public. We often hear the term "going public" bandied about, but what does it actually mean?

Going public basically involves taking the stock—or the shares—of your company and registering them with the stock market in order to sell those shares to the general public via stockbrokers and investment bankers.

As you might imagine, this opens your company up to an entirely different world of public exposure, as well as scrutiny. Public companies are held to a different standard, legally and technically, than private companies, and you should be aware of those differences. You should also be aware that as a cash-infusion method, going public is second-to-none.

Elite Entrepreneurs should understand this concept of "going public" because it is an excellent exit strategy, other than selling the company you've worked so hard to build.

Or, if you're in this for the long haul and feel you still

have things to accomplish with this company, consider going public with your *financial starting line*, as a way to infuse your company with cash.

I've taken three companies public so far, and I discovered it's a great way to raise capital. For example, we raised the capital for one company by receiving a $25 million term sheet (basically a non-binding agreement setting the terms of the investment) even though the company hadn't really done anything yet. Why? Because many investors were interested in the stock value of the company, not the company itself. I know that sounds harsh, but that's how the stock market works.

Think about it: Just because you have built this greeting card company, garden tool company, record label, or career coaching company from the ground up, most investors aren't necessarily interested in greeting cards, gardening, or hip-hop. They're interested in the potential of your company to either keep making money or make a lot of money in a sell-off.

Investors weren't there for the sleepless nights, the worry, the stress, the anxiety, the broken printing machine, the middle of the night alarms at your warehouse, the creative process, the recording sessions, the marketing or PR—and they don't want to be there! That's your job as an Elite Entrepreneur, to create this company that will eventually be worth something to somebody someday. That's the cold, hard truth of going public.

You have to consider why you're getting into this game before you walk onto the playing field. If you want to be merely a traditional entrepreneur, simply say, "I'll stay private and live the comfortable life." That's fine, and more power to you. If you want to be that type of lifestyle entrepreneur, close this book and give it to someone who wants to do something big. But if you want to be an Elite Entrepreneur and get the real money and do the real deals, then you're going to be dealing with the public market or selling your company to a public company.

If you want to be an Elite Entrepreneur and get the real money and do the real deals, then you're going to be dealing with the public market or selling your company to a public company.

Period. Of course, it's all about how you do the deal, and that's where Elite Entrepreneurs get creative.

GETTING CREATIVE WHEN
GOING PUBLIC

As an Elite Entrepreneur you likely have many ideas to nurture, avenues to explore, and passions to pursue. Going public allows you to exit one company and move on to the next by cashing out from the first to finance the second, and probably add some cash to your cache as well. I have started many companies, sold many companies, and look forward to starting—and selling—many more. You should, too.

Going public also puts you on the path to increased funds and can give you exposure to international markets, with access to even more capital. When you're public, liquidity and capital are far easier to come by than for a private company (i.e., a company not listed on the New York Stock Exchange or NASDAQ).

Of course, going public is more than a strategy; it is an official act that opens you up to additional responsibilities and regulations courtesy of the Securities and Exchange Commission. It also forces you to reveal potentially sensitive information concerning your operating expenses, finances, inventory, taxes, etc.

With greater exposure comes greater opportunity, however. Imagine your company's stock symbol on the NYSE or NASDAQ, along with Yahoo, Google, AOL, or Apple. The opportunity is real, and other than the reams of paperwork to file and legal hoops to jump through, it's much more accessible than you might think.

And don't think that the NYSE and NASDAQ are the only players in this game. Do you have to list your company in the United States? No. In fact, it's *easier* to list it offshore. Frankfurt, Toronto, London, Shanghai, and other cities around the world all have stock exchanges.

Again, it's all about being creative. While many companies get blinded by the image of Wall Street, don't limit yourself. Seek expert legal advice in this area and don't ignore the potential of going public on a foreign exchange in addition to, or even in lieu of, the NYSE or NASDAQ.

THE JOY OF LETTING GO

I know what you're thinking right now: "Ephren, I just started this company and already you're suggesting I sell it off to the highest bidder?" Well, yes!

Again, it's your choice, and if you're just starting up your company today, feel free to bookmark this page and return to it later. But when you do come back, I think you'll be more like me: seasoned, passionate, energetic, creative—but tired.

It's a lot of work running a company, work that doesn't always foster creativity. As entrepreneurs, we're ideas people. We come up with the concepts—the Pet Rock, the Chia Pet, the leopard print iPod phone cover, the risqué greeting cards.

As businesspeople, we're often stymied in our creativity because of the day-to-day details of managing the operation. Yes, there are people to help us do that, but at the end of the day, **if you just want to be another CEO sitting in the corner office, why call yourself an entrepreneur, let alone an Elite Entrepreneur?**

You have plenty more ideas, right? And not just gardening tools, greeting cards, or hit records. I started in video games, moved onto video production, got into finance, and now I'm doing things with oil, technology, digital, and cable. And each and every one of them is based on an idea.

Sometimes I come up with the idea; sometimes people bring the idea to me. Then I often rethink it or tweak it and maybe even combine it with another idea to make the original more marketable, more immediate, and, quite often, more profitable.

If I were still running every single company I'd ever started, I could never follow up on or pursue all these great ideas. Does that sound familiar? Does that sound like you? Then consider going public with your current company and get ready to take your *next* idea to the top.

THE BENEFITS OF GOING PUBLIC

There's a company I'm working with right now called Incoming. We actually took it public by doing a deal with Auctus Capital and raising about $25 million from them, all against the stock, and you know what? No credit check. No crazy bank documents. Just a quick little filing with the SEC and we began to draw out our money.

So if you're hesitant, uncertain, intimidated by, or even afraid of going public, reconsider that tired notion and look into it more fully. (For more about all of this, check out my Web site, www.eliteephren.com.)

Another interesting tale of a startup going public and succeeding (almost) overnight comes from a company called ZAGG, which stands for Zealous About Great Gadgets. This small, little-known company was producing a very singular product—a clear, scratch-proof cover for cell phones—for a very niche market.

But here, let them tell it (from the Zagg.com Web site):

"The first invisibleSHIELD™ design came about in early 2005 when a man wanted to protect his wristwatch from nicks and scratches. He found the solution in a clear, thin, and very durable military film originally made to protect US military helicopter blades from high-speed damage. He immediately saw the massive potential for a virtually invisible and indestructible protective covering in consumer use, and began working on two fronts: legally securing this new idea of putting clear protective adhesive film covering on electronic devices, and developing other innovative uses for the film. Once patents were prepared and filed, the invisibleSHIELD made its world debut.

"Over those first few months, positive reviews came pouring in and great word-of-mouth began to spread, one happy customer at a time. It started to become a phenomenon a few months later, in September 2005, when an invisibleSHIELD using this film was created for Apple's new iPod Nano. Sales of the new invisibleSHIELD design exploded online: it was literally becoming an overnight success. Robert G. Pedersen II (co-founder and CEO) knew that this idea and solution needed world-wide attention so on July 25th 2007, ZAGG Inc. went public and started trading under the symbol ZAGG

(NasdaqBB: ZAGG). The master plan was under
way. But that was just the beginning . . ."

Sound familiar? Going public doesn't necessarily mean you're getting ready to exit your company. It just means you're ready to move on to that next stage in the business cycle of your company. Maybe you need a cash infusion, maybe you're ready to share your product or service with the world, maybe you need the credibility—and publicity—of an NYSE or NASDAQ symbol.

No matter what the reasons, going public is a tried-and-true option for raising capital or setting your company up for a ripe sale or investment. The choice, as always, is yours.

PRIVATE MATTERS: A Word about Private Companies and Issuing Stock

Many people may not realize it, but public companies aren't the only ones that can offer stock. A private company can issue stock to equity investors who are coming in with money looking to invest. It's something that private companies can do, should do, and, frankly, might have to do to raise capital for their particular endeavor.

You're raising funds by selling equity in your company. In other words, with every "equity share" you sell, you are promising that investor a certain "share" of the eventual profits.

Naturally, as investors come in you need to be aware of regulatory rules and restrictions and should **seek legal advice**. But basically what you do is set up a "subscription agreement" and sell those shares to a particular investor who's interested in buying equity in your company. With the help of an attorney, you put together a Private Placement Memorandum to make sure everything is on the up-and-up. And you begin talking to accredited investors who will then become your "subscribers" by investing in your company.

Now, how do you find these accredited investors? There are conferences you can attend where you can pitch your company to a roomful of potential investors and meet and greet individuals who might be interested in buying equity shares. (Google search "equity investor conference" and you'll find dozens of these events, or better yet, visit www.eliteentrepreneur.com and let me do the work for you.)

Use these conferences as learning experiences. If you don't land any investors, don't be disheartened. What you are really after is the feedback about what you can do to make your business better. After all, these are conferences full of experienced businesspeople who have built and sold companies before, people who will tell you what you need to do to raise capital and attract investors.

I learned that lesson the first time I turned to one of my most important financial mentors for funding and he immediately said, "No." And believe it or not, that was the best thing he could have ever done for me!

He was right to turn us down, because at the time we weren't ready and we didn't have everything we needed in place. But he taught us how to package it so we would be ready and everything would be in place. And that's how we ended up eventually raising the money we needed—with a package that was right, a package that included everything a potential investor would need to have faith and confidence in our ability to use his money wisely.

That is the same formula I follow today.

LLC VS. C-CORP: A Quick Primer

As you begin to set up your company, there's one more important decision to make: What type of company it is going to be. For my money, all of my companies have either been a C-Corporation (or C-Corp) or an LLC.

- **C-Corp:** A C-Corporation is a general, for-profit entity so named for Chapter C of the IRS Code. In this scenario, shareholders "own" the corporation and the company is run by a board of directors.
- **LLC:** LLC stands for a Limited Liability Company. More flexible than a C-Corp, the LLC is not, in fact, a corporation but instead a company. This form is well-suited for companies run by a single owner (as is often the case with entrepreneurs).

I recommend the LLC business model because it gives you the best of both worlds. For one, the LLC is cheaper to administer than the C-Corp, yet it gives you the legal protection of a C-Corporation. The LLC is also easier to manage because there is less paperwork and fewer taxes. To my way of thinking, the C-Corp is more appropriate when you get ready to do more than $1 million in sales a year, because it gives you flexibility when you get prepared to actually go public.

ELITE ENTREPRENEURS AND EQUITY:
When to Keep It and When to Give It

Equity is the value of your company relative to debt. In other words, add up the company's assets and subtract the liabilities and what's left over is equity. Naturally, the more debt you have, the less equity is available, and the less debt you have, the more equity is available. You can use equity for contracts, consultants, vendors, partners, salespeople, etc.

When you own a public business, your equity is reflected in the amount of shares of stock you personally have in a company. In this case, the word "shares" is appropriate because when you offer investors, C-level employees, or even salespeople private-placement-memorandum-document-agreement "shares" of a company in the form of equity, you're inviting them to "share" in the company's profits. That's what's meant by an "equity share." Typically, owners have a controlling amount of shares of stock, which is the way they keep control of their company.

To me, equity is currency—just like cash. But you need to use it wisely. In other words, don't offer every employee equity shares in the company. There are only so many shares to go around. Otherwise, you could wake up one morning to find you don't own anything.

It's a little like putting on a rock concert with only 10,000 seats. Sure, you can print as many tickets as you want, but at the end of the day only 10,000 people are getting in. So if you give 500 tickets to this employee and 1,000 to that new manager you just hired, plus allow investors to eat up another 6,000, and then give an angel investor an additional 4,000 tickets, and . . . well, you've given away more tickets (shares) than there are seats (allotted shares). The event is now beyond sold out!

And, by the way, where are *your* tickets?

This is where entrepreneurs get in trouble; they use equity like cash, forgetting there is only so much to give out and that they have to retain some for themselves or they'll lose control of the company to someone else.

Remember this, Elite Entrepreneurs: **It's better to control a company than own a company.** What do I mean by this? Case in point: If you're careful with your equity, you can retain the majority of shares in your company (depending on what type of shares they are— we'd need a whole other book to cover the subject of share types). What good is it to control a company if you don't own it?

Owning something is in name only. You can own your company, but if you don't have the controlling amount of shares, that ownership is only as good as the letterhead your company name is printed on. Investors can do what they want with the company—restructure, reorganize, refinance, even sell—because they hold the controlling number of shares.

Unfortunately, many entrepreneurs cling onto their company, saying they "own" all of it, but since they don't have equity they don't really have a company. It's just them—a lifestyle business. Real entrepreneurs, Elite

Entrepreneurs, sell off pieces of their company in which they have equity to strategic partners. Together with their partners they then get the resources they need to take the company to the next level.

PARTING WORDS ABOUT CASH FLOW EXPLOSION

Yes, there is a lot going on in this chapter, and as I said in the beginning, entrepreneurs aren't always comfortable when dealing with money. The good news is you don't have to be.

I've talked at length about partners, and here is a good opportunity to partner with someone for whom money is as simple, free-flowing, and passionate as ideas are to you. (Yes, there *are* people like that out there!)

If this chapter gave you sweaty palms and nightmares, you may need financial help, and not just in terms of a huge cash infusion. But just as you seek out partners to help you print your greeting cards or machine tool your gardening equipment, look also for a trusted financial mentor to not only steer you through the confusion of going public or offering private stock, but to provide you general financial help as well.

Money matters, even if you're in this for the creativity, the passion, or simply the thrill of being an entrepreneur at the helm of a new startup. If you are an idea person, someone who can't be bothered or can't be trusted to run the books, get help and get help now. You'll be glad you did.

8

BUSINESS PHASE 7

CHAMPIONING CHARITY:

The Importance of Social Entrepreneurship

his isn't a chapter I would write for traditional entrepreneurs, but since you are an Elite Entrepreneur, let's talk about a way of doing business, indeed a lifestyle, that is very dear to my heart: social entrepreneurship.

Social entrepreneurship is essentially using business solutions to address the social ills of the community. We do it at City Capital by focusing on economic empowerment and self-sufficiency through job creation, biofuels production, etc. In addition to being an Elite Entrepreneur, I consider myself a social entrepreneur as well, and being a social entrepreneur is all about job creation and economic stimulation.

3 REASONS TO BE A SOCIAL ENTREPRENEUR

When you can build your brand and your company around supporting a charity or a movement or a cause, you give yourself a tremendous amount of leverage in three specific areas:

■ REASON 1: *Media Opportunities Can Expand the Audience for Your Product*

Becoming a social entrepreneur is just about the fastest way to become a local—even national—media sensation. And, between you and me, it's easy to do!

Let's say you run a company that makes shoes specifically for skaters. These shoes are edgy, black and red and white, with skull designs and different-colored laces and bottom treads that leave distinct impressions in the sand. "Tweens" and teens love these shoes—they can't buy enough of them.

That's great, but as we all know, kids are fickle and today's "must have" accessory is yesterday's fad. So what do you do to stay relevant and culturally aware? Look around your community and try to find a place that would welcome a few free pairs of shoes.

Consider a homeless shelter, a school shoe program, a church center, or other local organization that regularly deals with the underprivileged. Liaison with these folks to provide a specific number of pairs of shoes for free.

Maybe every year the local school system runs a "shoe drive" to equip underprivileged kids with shoes for the summer months. What a great opportunity to donate a few dozen pairs of your shoes to kids who will not only need them but, since they're so cool and edgy and hip, will actually wear them.

This is a great opportunity to put your social entrepreneurism to work *and* let the local media know what you're doing. After you finish one successful event or campaign, do more and more. They don't have to be big or costly to have a huge impact. Assign someone on your team to be your local media liaison, to not only handle requests from the press but to also actively look for additional ways to be a social entrepreneur.

■ REASON 2: *Opportunities to Become More Attractive to Partners*

Social entrepreneurism provides both credibility and clout on the local and national level. This comes in handy especially when your company is more mature and you are reaching out to strategic partners. Those potential partners will quickly notice social entrepreneurism efforts and know a lot about you as an entrepreneur, a leader, and, most important, as a person.

Never forget that while you are often seen as an entrepreneur, partners want to work with real people—and nothing says "real" like social entrepreneurism. And never forget that if you ever need government to get involved in your business or your community efforts, you'll have that required "pedigree" that comes from being involved with various local, national, and charitable organizations.

Let's say you're looking to partner with a local or national government agency on a certain product, service, idea, or initiative. Naturally, there is a pretty stringent vetting process. And let's say you regularly participate with and donate to charities such as the Red Cross, Salvation Army, Boys Club of America, the Girl Scouts, etc. Having these instantly recognizable organizations listed on your corporate Web site as "partners" will help government officials feel better about partnering with you as well.

■ REASON 3: *Opportunities to Expand Your Network*

When you look at the boards of directors of the organizations you support, partner with, or donate to, notice the titles next to the names. Let's say the boards of directors at your local Boys & Girls Club has twenty members; most of them will be CEOs, CFOs, presidents, vice presidents, and/or founders of some of your city or state's most influential corporations. Many of them run your local banks, law offices, or other private companies.

Now imagine handing out water bottles to runners in a local 5K charity run, standing next to a bank president in your company T-shirt. Or feeding the homeless on Thanksgiving, while the senior vice president for the city's best PR firm dishes out mashed potatoes next to you in the serving line.

These are very influential people, and working side-by-side with them as a social entrepreneur not only gives you instant credibility, it also makes you human to them. You aren't just a face and a name; instead, you're "that guy who donated all those shoes to my kid's school" or "the guy who stayed late on Thanksgiving to help clean up the pots and pans."

So definitely hang around the right charities and the right causes and the right events. It's good for the community, and it's good for you and your business.

SOCIAL ENTREPRENEURSHIP IS THE SECRET TO LONG-RANGE SUCCESS

Business isn't just business anymore. When all a company has to offer is products, it's just another company. Anyone can make a widget, a shoe, a soda, or a gardening tool. With so many choices on the market today, people really do "vote with their pocketbook."

Competition is so stiff that consumers can pick and choose where they get what they want, and often for how much. So how can you ensure their loyalty? By creating not just a company, but a purpose. You can't just create things; you have to stand for something, too.

When a company supports a cause and has a purpose that it believes in, that people can touch, see, hear, and feel, the community will be much more receptive to that company. In fact, the community will prefer that company's brand over others, regardless of whether the company's product is superior to others'. Having a purpose is one more way a company can insulate itself from some marketplace uncertainty and build what I call "drop-dead consumer loyalty."

People don't want to simply buy things anymore; they want to participate in some kind of movement. They want their dollars and cents to go toward something, not just another item for their closet or pantry.

Dell. Converse. Starbucks. Nike. Gap. Apple. Hallmark. These companies associate themselves with the (RED) Campaign to help fight AIDS in Africa. So every time you buy one of their specially designed red products—like Dell's custom-built red laptop or Converse's special sneaker or a Gap T-shirt—up to 50 percent of that product's profit goes straight to the AIDS fight in Africa.

This isn't just social entrepreneurism; it's buying for a cause. Am I necessarily a Dell customer? If I can get a great computer at a great price and know I'm helping save lives, I am now! And since I bought that one Dell laptop and it was a good one, I'm probably more likely to be "drop-dead loyal" to that product—and to Dell.

This is the power of social entrepreneurism and the reason why it's the future for Elite Entrepreneurs. Branding is so powerful, and if you can brand yourself as a social entrepreneur in this day and age, half of your marketing and PR work is done for you.

Branding is so powerful, and if you can brand yourself as a social entrepreneur in this day and age, half of your marketing and PR work is done for you.

And I'm not just being mercenary here; this is branding with a purpose. It's *business* with a purpose. So don't just attach yourself willy-nilly to charitable organizations because they're popular or "it worked for Dell." Look for causes that resonate with you. Maybe your wife is a cancer survivor, or your friend has diabetes, or you grew up poor and hungry or dropped out of school.

Now that you are a successful entrepreneur, you have an opportunity to give back. And much the same way as buying a (RED) product donates half the profits to a good cause, doing good work for good organizations is simply good business.

Now more than ever the world needs your help. Why not help yourself in the process?

THE HUMAN SIDE OF SOCIAL ENTREPRENEURSHIP

Social entrepreneurship has definitely made me more aware of community issues. It's gotten me far more politically involved, even to the point that I spoke at the Democratic National Convention and with local government agencies on policy issues. I never considered myself political until I got involved with in social issues via my companies.

Social entrepreneurship also keeps me informed about what's going on in my community, and I have made so many wonderful new friends at meetings, charitable events, concerts, 5K runs, church events, and so on.

I know I look at life differently these days, becoming much more of a global citizen. When I look at my life now, I feel fortunate, and it makes me want to do even more in my community, not less. It also affects my hiring decisions. I often think, is this person going to be a team player? Is he going to wear a pink T-shirt for Breast Cancer Awareness Month? Will he "get on board" with our various charitable activities? It doesn't make or break a new hire, but it definitely gives me pause when I come across potential employees or partners who are *not* active in the community.

PARTING WORDS
ABOUT CHAMPIONING CHARITY

If you remember only one thing about this chapter, remember these twenty inspiring words: **The only way that you can become a great Elite Entrepreneur is if you help others become greater than you.**

As I said at the beginning of this chapter, this is not a message I would share with traditional entrepreneurs. Why not? Because, frankly, they aren't all that interested in bettering themselves or, for that matter, leaving the world a better place.

Elite Entrepreneurs *are*—and that's what makes all the difference.

A few chapters back I told you most potential investors in your company don't care a whit about your cause, your passion, your family, your friends, your partners, or even your message; they care only about your company as an investment.

You could be a practicing Satanist for all they care, but if your company turns a profit or could make a quick buck in a fire sale, they're in. Well, the fact is, many entrepreneurs are like that as well.

They work hard because they are passionate only about making money. If they get a hot idea, it's because they know it can make them money. If they follow trends, it's only to see what isn't on the market and work to fill that gap and turn a profit.

And more power to them. I admit the prospect of making a buck makes me pretty passionate as well! (I bet it turns you on, too.) But having started and sold several companies by now, I know I could make it in any business, and that's why I choose only to do business with products, services, and people I feel passionate about.

What inspires me are the Elite Entrepreneurs I meet every day, every week, all the time. I give talks all over the country, at schools, college campuses, organizations, community centers, and churches. People come to hear me speak because, I believe, each of us has an Elite Entrepreneur inside of us, waiting to break out and make a difference

But what I see now more than ever is the young people of this country becoming entrepreneurs because they know it is the quickest, surest, and most-effective way to effect change in these challenging, uncertain, and anxious times.

I believe many young people are rejecting the corporate world and going into business for themselves. And at community centers and churches I often meet middle-aged people and baby boomers who are starting businesses because they're tired of the red tape and bureaucracy that corporations generate.

Now, I'm not dissing corporate America; I'm just reporting from the front lines of America today. As entrepreneurs, these people have the power to make their own decisions, to succeed or fail based on their own actions, energies, and enthusiasms. What's more, the very reasons they are getting into business have changed.

Of course I speak at "millionaire conferences" all over the world where the primary goal is to achieve great financial wealth. And hallelujah that we live in a free, capitalist society where that is not only legal, but encouraged! But I also hear many people who want to become entrepreneurs for one simple reason: to change the world.

That's it—they want to earn a living, but only in order to eat and sleep and keep working on their dream! These people are creating new ways to get drinking water to the world's underprivileged; they're revitalizing Books on Wheels programs in their local communities; they're revamping homeless shelters; they're providing leftover restaurant food to the hungry people.

I have heard more charitable and socially entrepreneurial ideas in the last five years than could fit in all the pages of this book. Every new idea I hear revitalizes my passion to share the wealth.

And, speaking of sharing, here is my message to you: Share this book. Pass it on. Don't just close it, stick it in your library, and forget about it. Give it to your spouse, your neighbor, your friend, your colleague, your mom, your dad . . . your son or daughter.

Better yet, buy them a copy as a gift; give it for birthdays, anniversaries, and holiday presents. Send them to my blog, forward the eBook to others, and share the message that **they, too, can be an Elite Entrepreneur.**

Remember, the only way to be great is to share greatness. Start sharing today!

CONCLUSION

By now I think it's pretty clear that Elite Entrepreneurs are something special, something . . . extra. Well, sure, that's what makes them "elite" in the first place. What kind of Elite Entrepreneur would I be if I didn't give you the opportunity to stay in contact with me and reach out to me for business mentorship and strategy sessions? You can reach me at www.eliteephren.com, where you will receive bonus advice from the book, information on events, and the opportunity to fly out to New York and sit down with me or schedule a call with me so I can help take you to Elite Entrepreneur level.

Becoming an Elite Entrepreneur may be difficult, but it is possible! Here are some common questions you may have been asking yourself before you started reading this book:

- Do I really need to raise a million dollars or do I need to spend money finding the right partner?

- Do I really need to go after this particular market or do I need to go after a smaller market, but be able to charge more by identifying a niche?

- Do I really need to focus on being the chief representative of the company or do I need to go higher and become that great rainmaker who is able to bring sales in?

- Do I determine ahead of time that I can actually sell my product first, or is all of this just a pipe dream about something that only I would buy?

- Am I hiring and surrounding myself with the right people?

- Does my brand represent what I really want to see for my company?

- Does the logo show that?

- Does our imagery show that?

- Is my company a movement or simply a movement of dollars and cents back and forth?

- Is it something people can get behind?

- Am I creating a brand that is really a campaign?

By now I hope I've answered those questions for you— and then some. The beauty of being an Elite Entrepreneur is, of course, that we find our own way. If Product A is incomplete, we find what we need in Product B or Product C. Business is a puzzle, and it's never quite finished, although the more experience you have in business, the more pieces you've managed to fit together.

I like to think that what I've created with this book is a kind of "best of" guide to all the tools you need to start your own company. Obviously, I couldn't include everything—for example, your state's tax code, the three hundred or so pages you'll need to read about starting your own LLC, and what it really means to go public on the stock market. But I believe I've given you something much better: the inside scoop on what that stuff really means.

Many of you came to this book with preconceived notions about what it means to be an entrepreneur, let alone an Elite Entrepreneur. One of those misconceptions, I believe, was that entrepreneurs really are their own bosses, that, in short, they are "free."

Elite Entrepreneurs realize that being an entrepreneur and reporting to nobody, having no accountability, and being your own boss is a complete myth. That is not a successful individual. Successful individuals who are Elite Entrepreneurs are the kind of people who are willing to be held accountable but are also willing to hold other people accountable as well.

In the end, particularly as social entrepreneurs, we realize that our freedom—our *true* freedom—comes from empowering other people and helping other people to become free. If you're like me, you'll probably never be truly free because there is always another idea to pursue, a dream to fulfill, an opportunity to speak, a charity event to attend, or a passion to fulfill.

Being an Elite Entrepreneur isn't easy. To start your own company, let alone make it successful, you will sacrifice your family time, your social life, your sports activities, your TV shows and movies, and in some extreme cases your health. You will gain pounds from all those late-night, to-go containers, or lose weight because you got so caught up in the moment you forgot to eat—again. And say goodbye to sleep, unless you set up a cot in the office!

But you know what? I wouldn't have it any other way.

And, chances are, neither would you.

That's because we understand that anything great worth having—or worth doing—requires sacrifice. And with the support of our loved ones, our friends, our business partners, and our strategic advisors, we are willing to do that to make our dreams come true.

Finally, I believe that if we are ever to achieve any kind of freedom in our entrepreneurial endeavors, we must hold this thought dear: **We Elite Entrepreneurs are willing to do what others aren't in order to spend the rest of our lives doing what everybody else wishes they could do.**

Entrepreneurs come and go. We all know plenty of

people with big ideas, people who are *going to* do this and *going to* do that. We also know that 99.9 percent of those folks will never get up off the couch long enough to do even 1 percent of what it takes to become successful.

I hope this book has been a good read for you, but a challenging one as well. I designed it that way. If you can read this book and still be passionate, purposeful, and committed to your dreams, you do have what it takes to become an Elite Entrepreneur. You'll never let anyone else tell you it's too hard out there to succeed.

You know the odds are long, the politics are stupid, the statistics are doom and gloom, but you still want to start that business. Good for you. Now it's time to put that energy to good use, and I wish you well on your journey. Statistics say only 2 out of 5 entrepreneurs succeed—and I want you to be one of them! As a thank-you for purchasing this book, I am offering you a special discount to www.2outof5.com, my premium membership Web site serving entrepreneurs of all ages and stages of development. The site will help you in your journey to be an Elite Entrepreneur. Visit www.2outof5.com and enter coupon code ELITE to redeem your special discount.

And as you begin the long and winding startup process, please do check in at my Web site, www.eliteephren.com, and let me know how it's going.

You never know, your inspirational story could just make it into this book's sequel!

ABOUT THE AUTHOR

Ephren Taylor II is a *Wall Street Journal* bestselling author and the CEO of two publicly traded companies, one of which is recognized by *The Wall Street Journal* as one of the "Top 100 Socially Conscious Corporations in the United States." Named by *The Michigan Chronicle* as one of the top "ten people making a global difference," the 27-year-old Taylor is the youngest African-American CEO of any publicly traded company in United States history. Taylor began his career as a videogame developer at the age of 12 and built a multimillion-dollar technology company by age 17.

As a *business accelerator,* Taylor oversees millions in assets while serving a diverse clientele of blue chip, private, and multi-tier branding development interests. He is engaged in building investor and shareholder value through socially conscious yet profitable investing that empowers urban communities. Thus far he's successfully developed multimillion-dollar initiatives ranging from creating affordable housing for working-class families to developing and producing biofuels. Through his green energy and philanthropic initiatives, Taylor is leading a new wave of CEOs focused on corporate social responsibility. Under Taylor's direction, nearly every company and initiative he has been involved with has experienced accelerated growth.

A nationally recognized authority on personal wealth and entrepreneurial business development, Taylor appears regularly on Fox News and CNBC and has been featured on network shows such as ABC's 20/20, Montel Williams, and many others. He also has had regular appearances in the print and radio media, including PBS, *Black Enterprise*, and the *Miami Herald*. Additionally, Taylor's name generates nearly 400,000 search results on Google.

Beyond his unprecedented accomplishments at such a young age, Taylor is an author, inspirational speaker, and business mentor.

His 2009 *Wall Street Journal* bestselling book **Creating Success from the Inside Out** (John Wiley & Sons) reveals the mindset of so many of today's multimillionaires, while defining success as not only attaining wealth, but also utilizing it. As a result, Taylor has become a frequently requested speaker and panelist at forums throughout the country.

Taylor has been called his generation's Warren Buffett or Jack Welch. What motivates Taylor the most, however, is the opportunity to spark new ideas and offer new solutions to problems that have plagued communities for years, decades, and even centuries.